NICCOLÒ MACHIAVELLI

The
Prince

Edited and Translated by
DAVID WOOTTON

Hackett Publishing Company, Inc.
Indianapolis/Cambridge

Copyright © 1995 by Hackett Publishing Company, Inc.

17 16 15 14 13   7 8 9 10 11 12

For further information, please address
  Hackett Publishing Company, Inc.
  P.O. Box 44937
  Indianapolis, Indiana 46244–0937

www.hackettpublishing.com

Design by Dan Kirklin

Library of Congress Cataloging-in-Publication Data

Machiavelli, Niccolò, 1469–1527.
    [Principe. English]
    The prince/Niccolò Machiavelli: edited and translated by David
Wootton.
        p.   cm.
    Translated from the Italian.
    Includes bibliographical references and index.
    ISBN 0-87220-317-4 (cloth)
    ISBN 0-87220-316-6 (pbk.)
    I. Wootton, David, 1952–   . II. Title.
JC143.M3813   1995
320.1—dc20   94-44698
                                                     CIP

ISBN-13: 978-0-87220-317-4 (cloth)
ISBN-13: 978-0-87220-316-7 (pbk.)

CONTENTS

MAP   viii–ix

INTRODUCTION   xi

FURTHER READING   xlv

LETTER TO VETTORI, 10 December 1513   1

THE PRINCE   5

Dedication   5

Chapter One:
How many types of principality are there? And how are they
    acquired?   6

Chapter Two:
On hereditary principalities.   6

Chapter Three:
On mixed principalities.   7

Chapter Four:
Why the kingdom of Darius, which Alexander occupied, did
    not rebel against his successors after Alexander's death.   14

Chapter Five:
How you should govern cities or kingdoms that, before you
    acquired them, lived under their own laws.   17

Chapter Six:
About new kingdoms acquired with one's own armies and
    one's own skill [*virtù*].   18

Chapter Seven:
About new principalities that are acquired with the forces of
    others and with good luck.   21

Chapter Eight:
Of those who come to power through wicked actions.   27

Chapter Nine:
Of the citizen-ruler.   31

Chapter Ten:
How one should measure the strength of a ruler.   34

Chapter Eleven:
About ecclesiastical states.   35

Chapter Twelve:
How many types of army are there, and what opinion should
    one have of mercenary soldiers?   38

Chapter Thirteen:
About auxiliary troops, native troops, and composite armies.   42

Chapter Fourteen:
What a ruler should do as regards the militia.   45

Chapter Fifteen:
About those factors that cause men, and especially rulers, to
    be praised or censured.   47

Chapter Sixteen:
On generosity and parsimony.   49

Chapter Seventeen:
About cruelty and compassion; and about whether it is better
    to be loved than feared, or the reverse.   51

Chapter Eighteen:
How far rulers are to keep their word.   53

Chapter Nineteen:
How one should avoid hatred and contempt.   56

Chapter Twenty:
Whether the building of fortresses (and many other things
    rulers regularly do) is useful or not.   63

Chapter Twenty-One:
What a ruler should do in order to acquire a reputation.   67

Chapter Twenty-Two:
About those whom rulers employ as advisers.   70

Chapter Twenty-Three:
How sycophants are to be avoided.   71

Chapter Twenty-Four:
Why the rulers of Italy have lost their states. 73

Chapter Twenty-Five:
How much fortune can achieve in human affairs, and how it is
to be resisted. 74

Chapter Twenty-Six:
Exhortation to seize Italy and free her from the barbarians. 77

INDEX 81

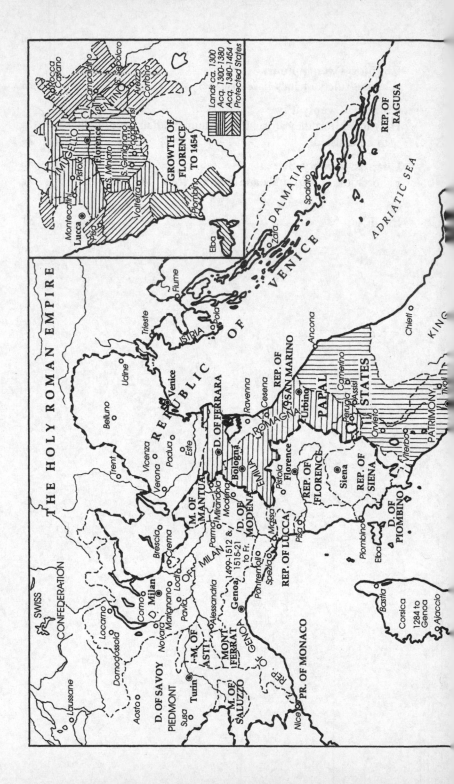

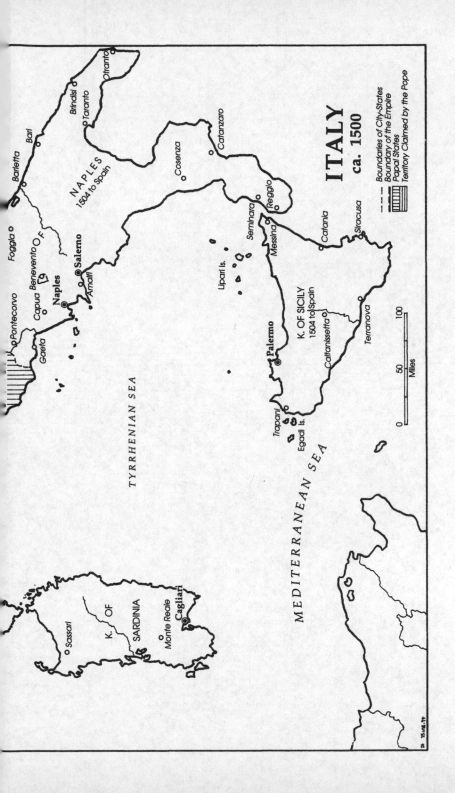

ITALY
ca. 1500

--- Boundaries of City-States
— Boundary of the Empire
Papal States
Territory Claimed by the Pope

NAPLES
1504 to Spain

K. OF SICILY
1504 to Spain

K. OF SARDINIA

TYRRHENIAN SEA

MEDITERRANEAN SEA

Pontecorvo
Gaeta
Capua
Benevento
Naples
Amalfi
Salerno
Foggia
Barletta
Bari
Brindisi
Taranto
Otranto
Cosenza
Catanzaro
Reggio
Seminara
Messina
Catania
Siracusa
Terranova
Caltanissetta
Palermo
Trapani
Egadi Is.
Lipari Is.

Sassari
Monte Reale
Cagliari

0   50   100
Miles

INTRODUCTION

As a method of torture, the *strappado* is simple but efficient. The prisoner's hands are tied behind his back; a rope is thrown over a pulley or beam; the prisoner is lifted into the air by his wrists. This is acutely painful and undignified, particularly if he is left dangling for hours or days. But from time to time he is dropped and allowed to fall a few feet before the rope goes taut; the sudden stop tears at his shoulders, even dislocating them. The pain is excruciating.

Torture was legal in most sixteenth-century states as part of the investigation of a crime. Machiavelli presented himself to the authorities, knowing what was in store, on 12 February 1513. Two acquaintances of his had been arrested for plotting against the new government of Florence, now controlled by the Medici family. In their possession was a list of names, of which Machiavelli's was one. He was presumably tortured fairly soon after his arrest—but not until he had heard the screams of other victims, and their cries of "Too high! Too high!" as they waited for the drop, for the torturer was not supposed to inflict permanent damage, and calculating the drop was not easy. Had he confessed under torture—and presumably people often confessed to crimes they had not committed—he would have been executed, as his two associates were. (One of them was, like Machiavelli, all too enamored of ancient Rome: he died begging the priest to help him get Brutus out of his head, so that he might die a Christian.) Machiavelli held out, in fact, through six drops and over several days. The torturers persisted longer than usual (four drops was the normal allowance), perhaps because they were persuaded he was guilty; or perhaps they felt his small, wiry frame had enabled him to get off lightly. In a letter to his friend Francesco Vettori, Florence's ambassador in Rome, Machiavelli was later to boast that he was proud of his own resilience.[1]

Was he guilty? We do not know. His torturers did not conclude he was innocent. Sixteenth-century Italian judges knew of degrees of guilt and innocence. One could be convicted, for example, of having given grounds for suspicion.[2] So Machiavelli was locked up. He wrote a poem to Giuliano de' Medici, who had once been a friend, asking, with what dignity he could muster, for him to arrange his release. His network of contacts was set in motion, in the hope someone had enough influence to come to his rescue. By good luck, as it happened, Cardinal

Giovanni de' Medici, Giuliano's brother, was elected pope, taking the name Leo X. On 12 March Machiavelli, along with all the other prisoners, was released. The prison gates had been thrown open so that even the most unfortunate could join in the public celebrations. But he was still confined to the lands of Florence, he was still under suspicion.

The lands of Florence: Draw a circle with a radius of twenty-five miles (forty kilometers) around Florence, and you will have a rough idea of the limits within which he was confined. Less than a day's ride from the city, and you would arrive at the frontier. Sixteenth-century Italy was divided into a patchwork of independent states, each linked to the others by a complicated and ever-shifting network of enmities and alliances. Forty miles to the south of Florence was the independent city of Siena; fifty miles to the north, the papal city of Bologna; rather nearer, to the west, and controlling Florence's trade routes down the river Arno to the sea, Pisa was sometimes independent, but now (since 1509, and thanks in large part to Machiavelli) under Florentine control. Three or four potentially hostile states were thus in a position to place an army outside Florence's walls within the space of a few days. Under such circumstances diplomats had to be constantly alert, and political and military advisers could never be sure what crisis they would face tomorrow.

Released from jail, Machiavelli retreated to his farm in the country. He could still see the dome of Florence's cathedral (designed by Brunelleschi in 1420) seven miles in the distance, but the city itself was small (perhaps seventy thousand inhabitants) and confined within medieval walls. The line between town and country was a sharp one, and Machiavelli was lost in the depths of the country. There, in the evening, he read his favorite authors, especially Livy, and he imagined himself dressed in a toga, an ancient Roman. This was not a very difficult feat of imagination, for farm life in the sixteenth century was not very different from life two millennia before. Hammers, saws and nails, plows and sickles differed little from their Roman prototypes.

Of course there had been some significant changes. Christianity had been the official religion of Italy for twelve hundred years, though Machiavelli seems to have had little faith in it: his friends teased him about his unbelief, and he joked to them about his failure to attend Church.[3] The printed book had been invented around 1440, but the full impact of the print revolution was only just beginning to be felt when Machiavelli was a young man.[4] He probably owned only a few books, for they were still expensive. He went to the trouble of transcribing long volumes for his own use: the entire text, for example, of

Lucretius's famous atheistical poem *De rerum natura*.[5] Wars were now fought with guns, though Machiavelli thought the military importance of gunpowder was greatly overestimated. The Battle of Ravenna, 1512, is sometimes said to be the first field battle whose outcome was decided by artillery.[6] And in 1492 Columbus had discovered the New World: Machiavelli compares his own discoveries in politics to the discovery of a new continent.

Of these differences the religious difference was, to Machiavelli's mind, much the most important. But more important than any differences were the similarities between his own city state and those of ancient Greece and ancient Rome. That he should have had such a strong sense of the relevance of antiquity is not surprising, for all the most interesting intellectual advances in art, in law, in philosophy, in medicine over the past hundred and fifty years had been grounded in the principle of imitating the ancients, of rediscovering lost techniques and forgotten ways of thinking. These discoveries were still going on as Machiavelli wrote: Tacitus's *Annals*, for example, were first published in 1515. The theories of Polybius to which Machiavelli refers in the *Discourses on the First Decade of Titus Livius* were normally available only to a few scholars who knew Greek. Since Machiavelli did not, he must have laid his hands on a manuscript translation or listened to Greek scholars describe Polybius's views.[7] For the intellectuals of Machiavelli's day progress was intimately linked to classical scholarship, for discovery was nearly always believed to be rediscovery. It was natural for Machiavelli to assume that, in his own subject, politics, the imitation of "my Romans," as he called them, was the path to follow.

In 1513 Machiavelli was forty-four. Of his life between 1469 and 1498 we know almost nothing, beyond the fact that his father was a poor lawyer ("I was born to penury") who went to some trouble to ensure that his son was decently educated. Machiavelli's father was probably illegitimate, which would explain why Niccolò was never entitled to participate in Florentine politics in his own right.[8] He was always an employee, never a politician. In 1498 when the radical, almost democratic, regime inspired by a reforming monk, Savonarola, was thrown into crisis and Savonarola himself was executed, there was a purge of government officials, and Machiavelli suddenly appears in the records as second chancellor of the Florentine republic. As such he was, from the start, a senior bureaucrat. The same year he was elected secretary to a key committee, the Ten of War, which meant he had much to do with military planning, with procurement and logistics.

As a civil servant, his most important achievement was the organiza-

tion, in 1505–6, of a militia, a Florentine conscript army to replace or
at least supplement the mercenaries on whom Florence, like other
Italian states, had traditionally relied. At the same time, Machiavelli
was frequently employed on diplomatic missions. He journeyed all
over Italy, made four trips to France, and one to the court of the Holy
Roman Emperor in Austria.

As a consequence of his professional experience, Machiavelli saw
politics from the point of view of the technician. His job was to predict
wars, preserve alliances, prepare defenses, raise taxes. Of wars there
was no shortage.[9] In 1494 Ludovico Sforza, ruler of Milan, had invited
the French, as his allies, to invade Italy. The French troops had swept
all before them (Machiavelli himself quotes the famous aphorism that
they had conquered Italy with a piece of chalk: the piece of chalk
that the quartermaster carried to mark the soldiers' billets) and had
discovered in Italy a land ripe for conquest, rich in plunder. The
resources of the little city states of Italy were no match for those of
the larger territorial states of France, Spain, and the Empire, while
Italian mercenaries were easily defeated by Swiss ones. For the rest
of Machiavelli's life, one foreign invasion was followed by another, and
the Italian states competed to find strong foreign allies. The trick was
to be the invader's ally, not his victim.

If the military defenses of the various Italian states had proved weak,
Italian governments were politically, as Machiavelli boasted, much
more skillful than their northern neighbors. For over a century five
Italian states (Florence, Milan, Naples, Rome, Venice) had been locked
in a struggle for dominance. They were used to forming networks of
shifting alliances and kept resident ambassadors (like Machiavelli's
friend Francesco Vettori) in the key cities to keep them abreast of the
latest developments. In these men's dispatches we can trace the growth
of the professionalized political skills that Machiavelli was trained to
deploy. Along with those skills came a particular set of moral values.
Around 1490 Ermolao Barbaro, Venice's ambassador in Rome, wrote
a little handbook for professional diplomats such as himself. "The first
duty of an ambassador," he says, "is exactly the same as that of any
other servant of a government, that is, to do, say, advise and think
whatever may best serve the preservation and aggrandizement of his
own state."[10] Machiavelli spent fourteen years faithfully serving the
Florentine state, thinking only about power, never, or hardly ever,
about principle.

Between 1494 and 1512 Florence's government was controlled by
a Great Council of three thousand citizens (perhaps twenty percent of

the adult males) who held office for life and could expect to pass it on to their children. The wealthy and influential resented the broad social basis of this regime, dismissing the majority of the Council's members as *popolani*, but, despite this hostility, the middling and poorer citizens gained increasing control after 1499, when appointments to the key committees that ran the city's day-to-day business began to be made by a process that gave an important role to selection by lot. These committees had a constantly changing, and increasingly inexperienced, membership, and in 1502 it was decided to introduce an element of continuity into government by the election of Piero Soderini to the new office of gonfaloniere for life. From the beginning the powers and role of the gonfaloniere were ambiguous, but the *popolani* seem to have gained more from his appointment than the elite.

Soderini believed in a policy of alliance with France, but in 1512 France proved unable to protect Florence from attack by the papacy and the Spanish (who possessed the Kingdom of Naples). Defeat at Prato led to the expulsion of Soderini and the return to the city, and to effective control of its politics, of the Medici family, who had governed Florence, while nominally being no more than private citizens, from 1434 to 1494. Early September 1512 saw widespread debate about constitutional reform among the Medici's supporters. On 17 September a coup d'état placed emergency powers in the hands of a large committee dominated by Medici supporters, the Balìa, and the Great Council was deprived of its powers. It was against this new regime that Machiavelli, who had been dismissed in November, was suspected of conspiring. In August 1513 Lorenzo de' Medici, nephew of the pope, arrived in Florence to take control, leaving his uncle Giuliano in Rome. On 22 November the Balìa agreed that in future routine power should be in the hands of a committee of seventy, although it continued to keep emergency powers in its own hands. Florentine government was thus nominally in the hands of a close-knit oligarchy, effectively in the hands of Lorenzo de' Medici. A few days later Machiavelli described to Vettori the first draft of his little book *The Prince*.

The first question we want to ask in reading *The Prince* is: What assumptions did Machiavelli bring to the study of politics as a result of his years of government service from 1498 to 1512? It is easy to show that *The Prince* draws largely on Machiavelli's personal experience (on his meetings, for example, with Cesare Borgia, the illegitimate son of Pope Alexander VI, who had conquered the Romagna in 1499–1501 and threatened to invade Florence), and key themes from it are already found in a letter known as the Caprices, written in 1506.[11] In particular *The Prince* lays great stress on the need for a ruler to establish a militia, and the formation of a militia had been Machiavelli's main personal achievement as a civil servant.

In recent years, however, particularly since an important article by Carlo Dionisotti, which first appeared in 1967, has begun to attract attention, there has been a good deal of disagreement among scholars about how to interpret Machiavelli's politics in these years of public service.[12] Dionisotti points out that some contemporaries saw Machiavelli as Soderini's personal agent, and feared that the militia would be used in a coup d'état to concentrate power in Soderini's hands. Two features of it were particularly disturbing. It was recruited from the countryside, not from Florence itself (it was thus not a *citizen* militia, but a *subject* militia),[13] and Don Micheletto, an extremely unsavory professional soldier, a former henchman of Cesare Borgia, and a specialist in strangulation, was placed in charge of it. We know from the *Discourses* that Machiavelli later felt that Soderini should have taken extralegal action to secure his hold on power and crush the supporters of the Medici.[14] One can thus argue that in the years before Soderini's fall Machiavelli's goal was the establishment of a dictatorship. If one takes this view, Machiavelli in *The Prince* was simply advising the Medici to do what he thought Soderini ought to have done. Machiavelli's later contempt for Soderini as a political baby would thus have been born of the conviction that he had missed an opportunity to seize power.[15]

Against this view it has been stressed that Machiavelli was a servant of the republic, not of Soderini. The militia was never answerable to Soderini personally, but only to committees on which his opponents were represented. In the *Discourses* (which some believe Machiavelli began to write in 1513) he appears as a committed supporter of republican, participatory government. These counterarguments have had considerable success in undermining Dionisotti's case, but it is difficult to believe Machiavelli was either an apolitical civil servant or an admirer of government by the Grand Council and its appointees. John Najemy has shown Machiavelli was in constant trouble for failing to keep the politicians properly informed of what he was up to.[16] One cannot help but feel his behavior suggests a professional civil servant's contempt for the amateurs from whom he was obliged to take his instructions, an attitude that could easily have led him to long for more authoritarian government.[17]

The second question we need to ask is: What was Machiavelli's purpose in writing *The Prince*? There is no doubt Machiavelli was seeking to gain employment from the Medici. He sent the manuscript of *The Prince* to his friend Francesco Vettori in Rome, saying that he was planning to dedicate it to Giuliano de' Medici, and asking for Francesco's advice on how to proceed. The conventional view seems to follow naturally: Machiavelli in *The Prince* was advising the Medici on how to govern Florence.[18] He hoped his advice would be recognized as good advice, and he would be offered employment, presumably with a view to putting his policy recommendations into effect. A minority view holds that the real position is much more complicated: Machiavelli knew the advice he was giving was bad advice, and he hoped the Medici, by adopting it, would bring about their own ruin.[19]

In my view both the conventional and the minority views are fundamentally misconceived. In fact, the real subject of *The Prince* is not Florence, and in it Machiavelli discusses Florentine politics only in passing.[20] A number of texts about how to govern Florence were produced during the crisis of September 1512 and during the months prior to the reform of November 1513. These canvassed a wide range of options, including dictatorial government. But if Machiavelli intended to write a text of this sort, he missed the boat. By December, the key decisions had been made. Moreover, if he wanted to be hired to play a part in the government of Florence, he was going about it the wrong way. By August 1513 it was clear Lorenzo, not Giuliano, was to be in charge of Florence, and it was he whom Machiavelli should have been seeking to contact, not Giuliano, who was far away in Rome.

In any case, *The Prince* fails to discuss the key problems that exercised those concerned with governing Florence. Their debates revolved around questions such as whether the pre-1494 constitution should be restored, whether the *popolani* should be allowed a role in government, whether the interests of the elite and the Medici were the same. Except for a brief aside in chapter twenty, Machiavelli is not, in *The Prince*, concerned with these practical questions.[21] It is simple to compare *The Prince* in this respect with a letter of advice to the Medici of 1512, the "Ricordo ai Palleschi," or with an essay Machiavelli wrote in 1519 or 1520, the *Discursus florentinarum rerum*, which is about how to restore republican government to Florence.[22] It is also hard to reconcile the claim that *The Prince* provides advice on how to govern Florence with Machiavelli's letter of early 1514 about Lorenzo's administration. There he praises policies sharply at odds with those recommended in *The Prince*.[23] Either this letter is hypocritical, or he thinks the question of how the Medici should behave in Florence is quite different from the questions discussed in *The Prince*.

The Prince is an essay on how a prince who is new to power should rule. But the Medici were not new to power in Florence in 1513. They were merely newly restored to power. They had an existing body of support, traditional policics, a party ideology. Their problems are not the problems Machiavelli is addressing when talking about new princes: Indeed, he never even mentions the history of the Medici family.

One response among readers who have recognized some of these problems has been to conclude that *The Prince* is about new rulers in general, that it is an abstract analysis, not a practical guide.[24] But there is a more convincing alternative that ought to be apparent to anyone who reads the letters exchanged between Machiavelli and Francesco Vettori in 1513 and 1514. Machiavelli may, in the autumn of 1513, have hankered after a job in Florence, but he knew he had virtually no prospect of getting one, because those in charge of governing Florence regarded him with suspicion.[25] His best hope of a job was in Rome, where the Medici pope was proving a liberal patron to Florentines and where he had a well-placed contact, Francesco Vettori. In December 1513 Vettori was hoping Machiavelli might be employed to accompany Cardinal Giulio de' Medici as legate in France, but this came to nothing.[26] A year later, in December 1514, Vettori arranged what looks very like a serious consideration of the possibility of hiring Machiavelli. Machiavelli was asked to file a report on what papal policy should be in the event of a war between France and Spain for possession of Milan—he recommended allying with France. The report was read by the pope and Giuliano de' Medici, but, as in so many cases when Francesco tried to place a friend, no job resulted.[27] A role in shaping papal foreign policy would have allowed Machiavelli to put his professional skills to work without there being much reason to suspect him of having opinions or interests at odds with those of the government — although Soderini had always favored an alliance with France, so Machiavelli was afraid his advice would not seem impartial.[28]

Both Machiavelli and Vettori believed, at the time *The Prince* was being written, that there was another possibility for employment. They assumed the pope—a young and vigorous man—would take the necessary steps to ensure the Medici family acquired an hereditary state.[29] In the summer of 1513, the pope was thought to have his eye on Parma and Piacenza. In the autumn, the talk was of the French helping him to seize Naples from Ferdinand of Spain in order to give it to Giuliano: Hence, one may suspect, the prominent place Ferdinand occupies in *The Prince*. In early 1515 the pope, no longer on good terms with the French, negotiated with Spain and the emperor to acquire Parma, Piacenza, Modena, and Reggio for Giuliano. Francesco Vettori's brother Paolo was to become governor of one of the cities, and Machiavelli evidently hoped to acquire employment there, too.[30]

It is this papal objective of acquiring a state for Giuliano that provides the context for *The Prince*. In it, Machiavelli offers advice that would be suitable for any ruler of a newly acquired principality in Italy. The advice had to be general, for Vettori had warned him there was no knowing what territory Giuliano would acquire.[31] But it had to be advice for someone coming in from outside to rule territory within which he had no preexisting power base, and, in all probability, territory that had no tradition of urban self-government to overcome. Chapters one to twenty-five of *The Prince* are thus an advice book for a papal brother about to acquire a state of his own. Machiavelli originally hoped, I believe, that he might end up with the job he soon argued Paolo Vettori should have, the job of overall administrator of a new territorial state. Indeed, Machiavelli was considered by Giuliano for an appointment in February 1515, but he was vetoed by Cardinal Giulio de' Medici.

There has been a good deal of speculation as to whether chapter twenty-six, an excited, rhetorical call to free Italy from the barbarians, was added later. It would seem it must have been, for two reasons. In the first place, Machiavelli's letters to Vettori of 1513 show no hint of a desire to drive the foreigners out of Italy, and we have already seen that in 1514 Machiavelli positively recommended an alliance with one of the foreign powers. In the second, only when it seemed clear that Giuliano was likely to end up with a state in North Italy could such a policy appear remotely realistic. We should therefore accept Hans Baron's argument that chapter twenty-six was written between January and August 1515, which is the only period when such an outcome seemed likely. After September 1515, when the French secured Milan by defeating the Swiss at Marignano, there was no longer any prospect of driving out the foreigners.[32] Finally, the Introduction, a letter to Lorenzo, postdates the rest of the book, which we know was originally intended for Giuliano. It must predate Lorenzo's election as Duke of Urbino in October 1516, since Machiavelli addresses him as *Magnificus*, not (as would have been appropriate in writing to a duke) *Eccellenza*.[33] Contemporaries (and many modern commentators) thought he was encouraging Lorenzo in his known aspirations to become sole ruler of Florence. But this seems unlikely, for soon after Lorenzo's death in 1519 Machiavelli advised Cardinal Giulio de' Medici that it would never be possible to establish princely government in Florence. It is much more likely Machiavelli was responding to news of the plans to make Lorenzo Duke of Urbino, which took shape in early 1516. *The Prince* thus appears to have been written in three stages: Chapters one through twenty-five were written between July and December 1513;

chapter twenty-six, probably in early 1515, when Machiavelli once again hoped for employment; and the dedication, in 1516.

At none of these stages was Machiavelli primarily concerned with Florentine politics. It is striking there are very few references to Florence and the Florentines to be found in *The Prince*. Remarkably, there are no references at all to the Medici until the final, prophetic chapter. Two chapters, however, look at first sight as if they are directly relevant to the situation of Florence in 1513: chapter five ("How you should govern cities or kingdoms that, before you acquired them, lived under their own laws"), and chapter seven ("About new principalities that are acquired with the forces of others and with good luck"). In addition, chapter nine ("Of the citizen-ruler": *De principatu civile*) is clearly about city government. On closer inspection, chapter five is about free cities that are annexed by an existing state. Since the Medici had no preexisting state, the chapter would hardly appear to be relevant to their position in 1512–13. Yet it is hard not to suspect Machiavelli is also hinting at the situation of the Medici as rulers of Florence. He offers three alternative policies: to leave a formerly free city a large measure of independence, and collect tribute from it; to govern it oneself; or to destroy it. He never discusses what would be involved in governing it oneself—precisely what he ought to have discussed if he was advocating princely rule in Florence—but instead advocates destruction as the only sure policy, for otherwise, no matter how much time passes, previously free cities will always rebel as soon as they see their opportunity. If *The Prince* is really about Florence, then this chapter implies Machiavelli has no useful advice to offer (for what would be gained by destroying the city?), and Florence will eventually win back her freedom. Rather than conclude, as some have done, that Machiavelli is deliberately giving bad advice (surely he would not be so obvious about it?) or writing a satire (why then propose presenting it to the Medici?), we ought to recognize that Machiavelli is advising the Medici to concentrate, not on Florence, but on their other, safer opportunities for territorial acquisition. And, indeed, many Florentines complained that this was exactly what the Medici were doing in 1513, that Florence was far from being their first priority.[34]

Chapter seven appears to be about the position of the Medici in Florence only if one imagines they had been put there by Spanish arms and were dependent on Spanish favor. In reality the Medici had deep roots of support in the city, had received only half-hearted support from the Spanish, and were certainly no longer dependent on them. This chapter is not about the position of the Medici in Florence in

1513, but about the position in which Giuliano might find himself in Naples.

Chapter nine, on the other hand, evidently does have Florence as its subject. But is its discussion of "the citizen-ruler" who is chosen by his fellow citizens about the Medici? The Medici were not officially rulers of Florence. Technically they were merely private citizens; in practice, it is true, they were Florence's rulers, but they had selected themselves for the position, not been elected. It was Soderini who had become a ruler by the favor of his fellow citizens, and what this chapter primarily provides is an analysis of Soderini's position.[35] Soderini had, as Machiavelli later complained in the *Discourses*, failed to act decisively against his opponents. It was he who should have followed the example of Nabis of Sparta. As advice to the Medici, chapter nine is almost useless, for it recommends that the citizen prince establish a power base in the populace, without discussing how the Medici should set about doing this. Above all, it insists it is almost impossible to transform elected office into absolute, hereditary authority, and, although it suggests there might be some policy that would enable such a ruler to consolidate support, it never says what this policy is. At the very moment when he seems on the verge of giving some practical advice, Machiavelli says everything depends on specific circumstances, and that he will therefore put the question to one side. Machiavelli, both here and in chapter twenty, may be criticizing the reforms of November 1513 by insisting on the need to build a popular power base, but such criticism was scarcely opportune, and he seems aware his recommendations will not be welcome (*e però si lasceranno indrieto*). In practical terms he is advising Giuliano to turn his thoughts elsewhere, if he does not want the Medici's position to be as temporary as Soderini's had been.

A key chapter any interpretation of *The Prince* must explain is chapter eight, "Of those who come to power through wicked actions." Throughout *The Prince* Machiavelli recommends what others would have rejected as wicked policies, for all that matters is success. Yet here he makes a clear distinction between effective policies and admirable ones. Agathocles of Syracuse and Oliverotto of Fermo are examples of rulers who are effective and, indeed, Machiavellian. But "one ought not, of course, to call it *virtù* [virtue or manliness] to massacre one's fellow citizens, to betray one's friends, to break one's word, to be without mercy and without religion." What distinguishes Agathocles from Cesare Borgia, whose example Machiavelli insists one should follow?[36] It is easy to show that Agathocles is not an ideal ruler, in Machiavelli's own terms. He does not simulate goodness, but then

neither does Borgia. He does not found a new order, but neither does
Borgia. In fact, it is clear he has every good quality Borgia has. He
has a good and loyal army (which means a great deal in Machiavelli's
scheme of things), and, like Borgia, he is an example of how cruelty
can be well used to win the loyalty of the population. He is no Philip
of Macedon, who treated his subjects like cattle, for we are told he
made every effort to ensure his subjects benefited in the long run.[37]
Why, then, is he not admirable? Victoria Kahn, facing up to the problem,
has cleverly argued that Machiavelli is here deliberately confusing or
testing the reader. By making his advice ambiguous, he is placing his
reader in the position of a subject, unable to make sense of his prince's
policies.[38]

Such an interpretation would be compelling if there were no real
difference between Borgia and Agathocles, but in fact there is one,
and a very simple one. Both Agathocles and Oliverotto destroyed free
states, murdering their friends and fellow citizens. This is the one
crime Machiavelli will not forgive. Where it is concerned, success is
irrelevant, for Caesar is no better than Catiline.[39] As he says in the
Discursus florentinarum rerum, "to establish a principate where a republic
could do well, or a republic where a principate would flourish, is
difficult, inhuman, and unworthy of anyone who wants to be thought
pious and good."[40] Machiavelli may appear to teach the immoral pursuit
of power by any means. In fact, he clearly teaches two sets of moral
values: one deals with relations between states, where only success
counts;[41] the other, much more complex, concerns one's dealings with
one's fellow citizens, where the means must be justified by the purposes
they serve.[42] To seize power, as Agis and Cleomenes did, in order to
strengthen the republic is admirable; to seize it in order to establish
a lasting tyranny, however benevolent, is shameful.

Machiavelli, I would suggest, is telling the Medici that if they were
to concentrate all power in Florence in their own hands by means of
a coup d'état the act would be shameful; they will have no difficulty
finding competent advice, if this is their intent, but he is not the man
for the job. In short, here he declares himself to be a principled
republican who holds the view that republics should not be forcibly
destroyed by their own citizens; in the next chapter he argues that
there is no pacific way for a citizen to acquire long-lasting power. The
conclusion is obvious: A new prince ought to seize territory that is
accustomed to princely rule. It is only the false assumption that Machiavelli in *The Prince* is advising the Medici to seize absolute power in
Florence that has prevented this chapter, whose meaning is clear
enough, from being understood.

A good deal of recent criticism has argued that *The Prince* provides deliberately bad advice, is satirical, or is so ambiguous it provides no clear guidance. These interpretations all presume the true subject of *The Prince* is Florentine politics. Placed back in the context of Medici concerns in 1513, Machiavelli's argument reappears as relatively straightforward: He is offering himself as an adviser to a future ruler of an as yet unspecified Italian state, a state to be acquired through papal influence. The temptation to read *The Prince* as if it were written about Florence is a strong one, because we know so much about Florentine politics in this period, and Machiavelli, of course, knew even more. But in 1513 Machiavelli had little prospect of employment in Florence, and he knew it. In *The Prince* he was intelligently pursuing his own interests, as well as trying to interpret theirs to the Medici in terms he had reason to believe they would find acceptable. Any other interpretation makes *The Prince* incoherent, ambiguous, self-contradictory, and unlikely to benefit either Machiavelli or the Medici.

One of the advantages of this interpretation is that it greatly simplifies the vexed problem of the relationship between *The Prince* and the *Discourses*. One view, which goes right back to the sixteenth century, is that *The Prince* is a manual for tyrants, while the *Discourses* is a book by a lover of liberty. How, then, to explain the relationship between the two? The simplest explanation would be that Machiavelli had simply changed his mind. But most scholars used to think Machiavelli wrote the two works at almost the same time. This view seemed almost inescapable, for *The Prince* appears to contain a reference to the *Discourses* ("I will leave behind me any discussion of republics, for I discussed them at length on another occasion"), while the *Discourses* contains references to *The Prince*.[43] So, it was argued, the *Discourses* must have been begun before *The Prince* and finished later.

Most scholars, consequently, argued that the differences between *The Prince* and the *Discourses* are not as great as they might seem. One view holds that *The Prince* does not advocate tyranny, but attacks it. This argument places great emphasis on chapter eight, which on most accounts appears as a peculiar exception to the overall thrust of the book. It also emphasizes that Machiavelli insists a ruler is only secure if he has the support of his subjects and that he urges him to pursue policies from which they will benefit.[44] Another view takes as its starting point Machiavelli's recurring preoccupation in the *Discourses* with dictatorial legislators who seize power in order to institute reforms and construct a long-lasting political order.[45] Matters would be straightforward if the prince was intended to be such a man. But Machiavelli never discusses in *The Prince* the problem of how to construct a political system that will depend, not on the *virtù* of one man, but on impersonal institutions. A third view argues that Machiavelli believes republics can only be established under favorable conditions. The absence of such conditions in Florence makes republican politics idealistic, princely politics realistic.[46] This view seems to be at odds with Machiavelli's own *Discursus florentinarum rerum,* which insists that, in a Florentine context, republicanism is the practical option. A fourth view argues that the underlying values of both books are the same, for what Machiavelli wants is a state capable of conquering others, whether the state itself be republic or tyranny.[47] This is clearly true, but it sidesteps the question of whether Machiavelli is advocating princely rule or participatory self-government for his fellow citizens.

In an important series of essays, Hans Baron argued that *The Prince* and the *Discourses* were indeed incompatible, but the simplest solution was after all the right one: Machiavelli had written *The Prince* first and then the *Discourses,* changing his mind in between.[48] Internal evidence shows the bulk of the *Discourses* was written around 1517.[49] Machiavelli, in his foreword, says he would never have written the *Discourses* but for Zanobi Buondelmonti and Cosimo Rucellai, and we know he did not meet them until 1515. Cosimo died in 1519, so, since one does not write letters, even letters of dedication, to the dead, the work as we have it must have been written between 1515 and 1519. For 1513, when we know Machiavelli was working on *The Prince,* we have Machiavelli's extensive correspondence with Vettori. Had he been working on another project at around the same time, he would surely have mentioned it. In Baron's view the conclusion is simple: *The Prince* was written, with the exception of the foreword and the last chapter, in 1513; the *Discourses* after 1515. The crucial sentence in *The Prince* that appears to suggest otherwise can only be a later interpolation, added in 1516 when Machiavelli wrote the foreword dedicating the book to Lorenzo.

I happen to think this argument is fundamentally correct, but I want first to point out that the interpretation of *The Prince* that I have defended provides an alternative way of reconciling *The Prince* and the *Discourses.* If *The Prince* is not about how to acquire power in a free city, then it is perfectly possible Machiavelli could have written it while at the same time writing a book in praise of republican politics. He could quite reasonably hold that feudal Naples and bourgeois Florence would benefit from quite different sorts of government.[50]

Baron is right to insist there is nothing about the *Discourses* to suggest any part of it was written by 1513. Must we then conclude that the key sentence in *The Prince* that suggests otherwise (*"Io lascerò indrieto* *el ragionare delle republiche, perché altra volta ne ragionai a lungo "*)* is an interpolation? Commentators have been nearly unanimous in taking this to be a reference to the *Discourses*, and all have agreed it is a reference to a written work. But this need not be the case.[51] Machiavelli was writing for Giuliano de' Medici, who was, he believed, favorably disposed towards him, and Giuliano knew full well that Machiavelli was suspected of being an enemy of the Medici government in Florence, had been tortured, and had recently been released from prison. Machiavelli, one might suspect, would have felt obliged to acknowledge this problem, if only to deflect criticism. Our sentence does not say Machiavelli had ever written about republics, merely that he had discussed them. And it insists he wants to leave this discussion, not to one side, but behind: What is past is past. What discussion of republics could Machiavelli have been thinking of, a discussion that, in the winter of 1513, he was unquestionably eager to consign to oblivion, but bound also to acknowledge? A discussion that had gone on too long? The answer is so straightforward that I am puzzled no one has thought of it. The discussion Machiavelli is referring to is the one that took place as he dangled at the end of a rope in the city jail. What were his interrogators interested in, if not his attitude to republics, and his commitment to the republican cause?

This one sentence, which has misled generations of scholars, was, I suspect, originally intended as nothing more than a wry, private joke on Machiavelli's own ill fortune. Indeed, Machiavelli felt a compulsive need, in the autumn of 1513, both to reenact his own torture by catching birds in snares (an activity he describes as *dispettoso et strano*, which I have translated as "nasty and peculiar"), and to joke about what had happened to him. For example, in the sonnet he sent Giuliano in 1513 accompanying a gift of thrushes caught with his own hand, he apologizes for the fact that the birds are scrawny, but adds that his own scrawniness had not prevented the interrogators from getting their teeth into him.[52] And to Vettori he writes, "This letter of yours terrified me more than the rope."[53] In *The Prince*, putting a brave face on things, he talks, not of his tortured body or the rope, but of reasonable discussions about abstract problems in political theory: But he expects Giuliano to understand at once what he is referring to.

Buondelmonti and Rucellai were members of a group that met to discuss politics and history in the *Orti Oricellari*, the gardens owned by the Rucellai family, a group of wealthy young men with anti-

---

*"I will leave behind me any discussion of republics, for I discussed them at length on another occasion."

Medicean and republican commitments (Buondelmonti was to be condemned to exile after the failure of a plot to murder Cardinal Giulio de' Medici in 1522). The praise of freedom in the *Discourses* is exactly what we would expect in a work written to be discussed in such a circle. If Machiavelli was not a committed republican in 1513, he clearly was one in 1517. But this leads to another problem that has not attracted the attention it deserves, that of Machiavelli's intentions in writing a work that appears alongside *The Prince* in its earliest editions, the *Life of Castruccio Castracani*. While on a visit to Lucca in 1520, he wrote this brief biography of Castracani, a Lucchese tyrant who had made extensive conquests in the early fourteenth century.

The *Life* is a puzzling work in two respects. In the first place, much of it is fiction, not fact. Machiavelli invents the story that Castracani was a foundling, reared by a priest; he denies Castracani had children, when in fact he had many; he fabricates accounts of battles in order to illustrate the theories of his *Art of War*. These fictions might escape a reader unfamiliar with the details of Castracani's life, but, as if to incite the reader's suspicions, Machiavelli ends the *Life* with a long series of aphorisms that he attributes to Castracani, but that come for the most part from well-known classical sources. That these had been imported into the story from elsewhere was apparent to his first readers, members of the Rucellai circle.

Second, the *Life* offers nothing but praise for a man who had, in fact, seized power in Lucca from her citizens, destroyed the republic, and (on Machiavelli's account) massacred his fellow citizens in cold blood. Castracani thus appears as another Agathocles, and the *Life* is often compared with *The Prince* as an essay in praise of successful tyranny. Had it been written at the same time as *The Prince*, this would be bound to affect our interpretation of that work; as it is, it seems a very strange book for the republican author of the *Discourses*. Castracani so wants to be like Caesar that he is even keen to die like him; in the *Discourses* Machiavelli had expressed nothing but contempt for Caesar.[54]

Fortunately, a fairly straightforward explanation is available. By 1520 Machiavelli had established himself in literary circles as the author of *Mandragola* and *The Art of War*. His friends continued to seek employment for him with the Medici, as his financial needs continued to be pressing. Their plan in 1520 was to arrange for him to be hired to write a history of Florence.[55] In writing the *Life* Machiavelli must have been primarily concerned to show he could indeed write a history, something he had never done before. But secondly, he had to face the fact he still had a reputation for moving in anti-Medicean circles. He needed to find some way of demonstrating that he would not turn a history of Florence into an attack on the Medici. When, during his visit to Lucca, he came across the life of Castracani written in 1496 by a Lucchese citizen, Nicolao Tegrimi, he must have been delighted to see a simple solution to his problem. Tegrimi was an ardent republican, but he had written in praise of a despot as an indirect way of flattering the Sforza Dukes of Milan, Lucca's allies, to whom he had been appointed ambassador.⁵⁶ Machiavelli set out to imitate him by using praise of Castracani to indicate the flexibility of his republican values. At the same time, though, by clearly indicating that his history was fiction, not fact, he distanced himself from the views expressed in it. If Castracani was a fiction, might not the narrator also be an invention?

On this interpretation, the *Life* is not an honest presentation of Machiavelli's views, which are much more clearly expressed in chapter eight of *The Prince*. Rather it is a parody of the more cynical of Machiavelli's arguments, as is *Mandragola* (where a young man, assisted by a cunning adviser, tricks an old man into letting him sleep with his wife). Machiavelli is amusing himself by portraying "Machiavellism" in its most blatantly immoral form. *The Prince*, I have argued is not a satire; the *Life*, however, comes close to being one. But we may suspect that Machiavelli took little pleasure in distorting his convictions in order to curry favor.⁵⁷ Borrowing from Diogenes Laertius, he reports that Castracani once spat upon someone who sought a favor from him. The courtier's response was, "Fishermen are prepared to get soaked with seawater in order to catch a tiny fish; there's no reason why I shouldn't get soaked in spit in order to catch a whale."⁵⁸ Machiavelli, trying to curry favor, must have felt plainly how shameful his own position was.

Shameful or not, the strategy succeeded. Machiavelli landed the job of historian of Florence, a project on which he worked until he presented the completed volume to Giulio de' Medici, by then Pope Clement VII, in May 1525. Although written under Medici patronage, there was little need for Machiavelli in the *History* to compromise his principles to the extent that he had done in the *Life of Castruccio Castracani*. As he explained to a friend, he simply had to place his criticism of the Medici into the mouths of their opponents.⁵⁹ By this elementary expedient he could write for Medici consumption a history that made clear why one should be hostile to their rule, and could be read with pleasure by his anti-Medicean friends. Unfortunately, though, the fact that he had been a beneficiary of Medici patronage was to count against him when, in 1527, the Medici were overthrown. Machiavelli died that year, still denied any position of political significance.

I have argued so far that *The Prince* was largely written in the second

half of 1513, when Giuliano was expected to acquire a new state of
his own to rule. The *Discourses* was written later, between 1515 and
1519, and is concerned with republican self-government. These arguments are at odds with the traditional view, which holds that *The Prince*
and the *Discourses* were written more or less simultaneously. They are
also at odds with the generally accepted belief that both address the
problems of Florentine politics. Most scholars assume both works were
intended to be taken seriously, but some believe *The Prince* is a satire,
while others hold that Machiavelli is deceptive and disingenuous
throughout his work.[60] This latter view seems to me hardly plausible
as an account of works written for private circulation, not for publica-
tion, but I have suggested that there is something distinctly fishy about
the *Life of Castruccio Castracani*.

I want now to turn to a question that has much exercised scholars
in recent years, that of Machiavelli's language. In order to understand
Machiavelli, we need to bear in mind that his vocabulary for discussing
politics is very different from ours. Sixteenth-century Italian has no
words for "selfish" or "selfless," for "egotistic" or "altruistic," for
"anarchy" or "alliance."[61] It does not even have a word for "politics"
as we understand the term. By "politics" Machiavelli's contemporaries
mean the theory of good government, usually of a city-state.[62] For the
policies required to seize or secure power they use the phrase "*l'arte
dello stato*," or statecraft. But Machiavelli has words or phrases that
enable him to discuss most of the issues we want to discuss when we
talk about politics (and where necessary he can invent a phrase, such
as "self-charity" for selfishness), and it would often be artificial to
avoid using modern terminology when translating him into twentieth-
century English.

However, there are a number of words Machiavelli uses that at first
sight appear easy to translate, but are in fact problematic. The first we
should note is *principe*. Machiavelli's title is always translated *The Prince*,
but by *principe* Machiavelli never means a king's son. His term usually
means "ruler" (so that the book ought to be called *The Ruler*), and a
principato is any system of government where power is concentrated
in the hands of one man (e.g. monarchy, tyranny). But Machiavelli
sometimes uses the word to mean "leader," so the general of an army
can be *un principe*, as can an elected official in a republic; and he also
occasionally calls the Medici, who held no official position in Florence,
but for long periods of time effectively controlled its politics, "princes,"
meaning "de facto rulers." A republic can be *principe di se stesso*, i.e.
self-governing. Machiavelli's "princes" have "states." When he is dis-

cussing a king as head of state, or as ruling over a state, or when he is talking about statecraft, this presents no problems. Sometimes Machiavelli uses *stato* where we would use "government" or "power," to talk, for example, of a new government, or acquiring power. But *stato* sometimes means something closer to status: The Medici were not heads of state, but they had *uno stato*, a particular, private power, authority, status within Florence. To be *un principe* is to have *un stato*, but Machiavelli uses both terms to cover a wider range of cases than our terms "ruler" and "state."

In approving of someone, Machiavelli standardly refers to their *virtù*. By this he does not normally mean virtue in a Christian sense, for he has little time for humility or chastity. It might be thought his virtues are pagan ones, and he is surely aware of the origin of the word in *vir*, man. His virtues might be expected to be the manly ones of courage, prudence, temperance, honesty, and justice. But this is not the case. Machiavelli approves of rash actions when they are successful; he advocates the stratagems of the coward when they are necessary to ensure survival or are likely to lead to victory; he believes rulers must be prepared to lie, murder, and act unjustly. They must therefore master the arts of deception, appearing to be one thing while in fact being another, cultivating a public image at odds with the facts. In taking this view Machiavelli is deliberately going against the arguments of Cicero, who had insisted honesty, justice, etc. are always the best policy.[63] Machiavelli's virtuous man is much nearer to being a virtuoso (and *virtuoso* is, of course, the adjective in Machiavelli's vocabulary, *virtù* the noun). Just as a virtuoso violinist can play music that defeats others, so in Machiavelli's world a virtuous general will win battles others would lose, a virtuous politician secure power where others would lose it. Virtue is thus role-specific: Virtuous soldiers are strong and brave, virtuous generals intelligent and determined. The virtuous man is the man who has those qualities that lead to success in his chosen activity.

The virtuous man will know when to seize his chances and will recognize what needs to be done. He will identify opportunities where others see only difficulties, and recognize necessity where others believe they have freedom of choice. But even virtue cannot guarantee success: He may be unlucky, circumstances may change, someone with greater virtue may get the better of him. Virtue thus finds itself in a constant struggle with fortune. The wise man limits the scope of fortune by taking appropriate precautions, but he also recognizes that bold, apparently rash actions often pay off. If *virtù* is in part the quality of manliness, then fortune is a woman who can be mastered. This is Machiavelli's way of saying that nothing succeeds like success and that one makes one's own good luck.

Machiavelli, however, unlike these aphorisms, is offensive, and deliberately so: Modern readers notice only the violence between man and woman in chapter twenty-five of *The Prince*, but sixteenth-century readers would have been acutely conscious that fortune is a *lady* and would have been particularly shocked at the violence between social inferior and superior.[64] It would be wrong, I think, to jump too quickly from Machiavelli's gendered language to a simple reading of Machiavelli as a patriarchal chauvinist.[65] If anything he seems to be exceptionally prepared to recognize that women can legitimately exercise power. Lucrezia is the hero of *Mandragola*, capable, indeed, "of ruling a kingdom."[66] *Clizia* can be read as a critique of masculinity, and as portraying "a protofeminist community."[67] Machiavelli seems to have nothing but admiration for the Countess of Forlì, who, ruthless as any man, is prepared to sacrifice her children in order to hold on to power.[68] Given this wider context, it is perhaps worth remembering that when he wrote *The Prince* Machiavelli had himself recently been beaten and abused. Usually he portrays Lady Fortune as mastering him, not he her. Fortune, like the thrushes he captures, embodies not Machiavelli's sense of masculine power but rather his experience of powerlessness. It is not surprising, then, that she also evokes fantasies of revenge.

Success, mastery of fortune, is important, but not all ends are worth pursuing, not all means justifiable. Machiavelli's virtuous man seeks not merely fame, but glory. There is nothing glorious or virtuous about unnecessary cruelty and bloodshed; on the other hand, a squeamish distaste for violence may make things worse in the long run. Machiavelli thus advocates "an economy of violence."[69] Since history reflects the views of the victors, success, even if it involves murder or treachery, is likely to lead to glory, not infamy. There are some goals, however, that are in themselves shameful. No one should want to destroy good government in order to establish anarchy or tyranny; no one should want to be Caesar. Politicians should all aspire to establish sound government that enables the mass of society to live in security. This is the best recipe for success, but also the only goal that is morally admirable.

Machiavelli thus aspires to the creation of order; the term *ordini*, meaning those constitutional provisions and institutional arrangements that make stable government possible, runs as a recurring refrain through the *Discourses*. To establish and preserve government, however, "extraordinary" measures are often necessary: Rulers, and even private individuals, may have to act outside the law in order to restore good government or ensure stability. If Machiavelli believes strongly in the sort of order that makes justice possible, he does not believe one must always act within the law.

Virtue and fortune, opportunity and necessity, shame and glory, constitutional order and extraordinary measures: These are the key polarities around which Machiavelli's thought revolves, and many of the tensions in his work come from his attempts to balance them, one against the other.[70] But there is a further preoccupation that lies at the heart of the *Discourses*, a preoccupation with liberty. Orderly government provides what Machiavelli sometimes calls *il vivere civile* or *il vivere politico*. Kings can provide this; indeed, Machiavelli repeatedly praises France, where royal despotism and aristocratic tyranny are kept within the law by the *parlements*. This is the least one can hope for, although it is more than can be found in a tyranny or despotism. But better still is *il vivere libero*, or self-government.[71] Most men, the *plebs*, want only security. A minority, the *popolo*, those who are true citizens, want to participate in political life. A few, the *grandi*, want to be leaders. Where there is great social inequality, particularly where the *grandi* are a landed aristocracy, with castles and armed retainers, popular self-government is impossible. But where there is a reasonable degree of equality, where the wealthy and privileged do not have things all their own way, then, in a city-state, popular self-government is possible, and wherever it is possible, it is desirable.

Machiavelli writes eloquently about the superiority of popular self-government to the rule of one man. The people, he believes, are a better judge than any individual, and where there is freedom, prosperity follows. Above all, the people can change their leaders to adapt to changing circumstances. No other system of government is thus as well placed to adapt to changes in fortune. A virtuous people has those qualities that make self-government successful: courage, self-sacrifice, integrity. At this point it seems Machiavelli's cynicism is turning into idealism.[72] But it must always be remembered that Machiavelli believed people were easily corrupted and always inclined to be selfish. No system of government that relied on altruism could hope to succeed, even where young people were trained from childhood to seek glory in public service and avoid shameful behavior at all costs. Indeed, Machiavelli has very little to say about obligations and duties, for the simple reason that he does not expect people to take them very seriously.

What, then, makes successful self-government possible? Machiavelli's answer to this question was profoundly original. It was, he believed, the clash of interests, particularly the clash between the interests of *grandi* and *popolo*. As long as individuals pursued genuine collective interests, not merely private ones, good government could result, even if the collectivity with which they identified was only one social group within the city. In his *Discourses* Machiavelli broke new ground by approving of the conflicts between the senate and the people in Rome; in his *History of Florence* he placed a new emphasis on the guilds as the legitimate representatives of interest groups, and he even expressed sympathy with the revolt in 1378 of the *ciompi*, the poorer workers whose interests were not adequately represented in the guilds.[73] Machiavelli consequently views conflicts that are founded in divergent economic interests and differing social statuses as inevitable, and indeed healthy. Where these conflicts result in a balance of power and a mixed constitution, something resembling the general good, *il bene commune*, will result, and selfish, short-sighted individuals will end up behaving like virtuous citizens.

Florentine history was certainly a history of internal conflict.[74] Why, then, had Florence proved a miserable failure, while Rome had experienced success on a scale unparalleled in history? Machiavelli's answer to this question depends on distinguishing between productive conflict and destructive conflict. What he terms *sette* (sects, parties, factions) unite individuals across economic and status groups, appealing to supposed issues of principle (in Florence, Guelfs versus Ghibellines, and supporters of the Medici versus opponents). Such conflicts resulted merely in pork-barrel politics, in the attempt to monopolize the benefits of political power for an unrepresentative minority. Members of political factions might think they were seeking a greater good, but in fact their actions always proved in practice to be narrowly corrupt and self-interested. Machiavelli sees conflicts between factions as destructive, while conflicts between classes are constructive.

Machiavelli thus held that, under the right conditions, successful, virtuous self-government was possible, although it was bound to be accompanied by conflict, tumult, and the occasional resort to extraordinary measures. Machiavelli's cynicism legitimized a cautious optimism, but it is important to recognize the narrow limits within which he was optimistic. If the clash of interests within a city could have beneficial consequences, Machiavelli could see no way of mediating the conflict of interests between states. Governments would always be driven to go to war against each other. A successful city would be one well prepared for war. Since attack was the best form of defense, the liberty of one city would necessarily be based on the servitude of others.[75] At the best, conquered cities might enjoy a limited *vivere civile*, like the subjects of a monarch. Freedom could be the privilege of no more than a few. In the clash of city against city, state against state, only the fittest could hope to survive. In Rome the energy generated by internal conflict had spilled outward to fuel external conquest. Only such a martial liberty was worth having. Participatory politics was possible only where there was also military discipline. Machiavelli, who had seen cities looted, crops burned, and populations starving, could imagine no alternative to a world of wars and rumors of wars.[76] The trick was simply to be on the winning side.

Machiavelli is a brilliant author, and we need to give some thought to the way he presents his views in his work. Both of Machiavelli's major works, *The Prince* and the *Discourses*, begin with references to artists, and Machiavelli clearly believes there is a point of comparison between his own science of politics and the art of his day.[77] *The Prince* begins with Machiavelli comparing himself to an artist painting a landscape in which mountains rise from the plain: Only from a distance can you see the shapes and forms of the land. Machiavelli is writing almost a century after the discovery of perspective, and Machiavelli's artist is painting depth and distance. One should compare the painting of Machiavelli's own day with Machiavelli's insistence that he does not want to write an ornamental, decorative prose; instead he wants to portray the facts as they are.[78] Just as one looks *into* a Renaissance painting, seeing a world one feels one could step into and move about in, rather than regarding the painting as a decorative surface, so Machiavelli wants you to think of his books as windows on the world of politics. *The Prince* is intended to be like the bird's-eye maps Leonardo da Vinci drew for Cesare Borgia, enabling him to envision his newly conquered territories. Here, laid out before one, are the routes along which troops may advance, here the natural strongholds toward which to retreat when under attack. Machiavelli probably knew these maps and marveled at them.[79]

Machiavelli only once names an artist in his works. In *The History of Florence* he praises the great architect and sculptor Brunelleschi.[80] Brunelleschi had been involved in a plan to divert a river in order to cut off the city of Lucca so it could be the more easily besieged. The plan had been a dismal failure, as had Machiavelli's own attempt—on which he worked in collaboration with the greatest of all artist-engineers, Leonardo himself—to divert the river Arno in order to cut off Pisa from the sea. But I do not believe Machiavelli admired Brunelleschi simply because he was a military engineer (he uses of him his highest word of praise, *virtù*, which he normally applies only to politicians and generals). Brunelleschi's sculptures were supremely lifelike, so that, looking at them, one could forget one was looking at works of art and imagine one was looking at real people. So, too, Machiavelli aims to conceal his own artistry behind the appearance of realism. Realism, of course, is as much a contrived effect as any other, for the appearance of fidelity to nature is itself an illusion. But in order to achieve this effect, Machiavelli writes always about people and actions, rarely about authors and words. His *Discourses on Livy* have little to say on Livy, for what interests Machiavelli is Roman politics, not Roman authors.[81]

Machiavelli had been educated as a humanist, and conventional humanism was a discipline centered upon texts. Great authors were imitated, quoted, and paraphrased, learning paraded. Machiavelli expects his readers to have a humanist education and to recognize implicit references to Cicero or Dante. The core of a humanist education was the study of rhetoric, and students practiced rhetorical figures until they became second nature. Machiavelli would expect his readers to recognize that chapters sixteen to eighteen of *The Prince* are a virtuoso exercise in *paradiastole,* the redescription of behavior in order to transform its moral significance.[82]

Many humanists before Machiavelli had written essays on how to educate a prince, essays in which they displayed their learning and rhetorical skill and urged the prince to become, like them, learned and eloquent. Machiavelli is different. Both *The Prince* and the *Discourses* reject the humanists' preoccupation with the text and with it the humanists' concern with rhetoric, the art of persuasion, as the supreme political skill.[83] Of course Machiavelli often reports the speeches of politicians and generals, and acknowledges their importance, and *The Prince* echoes with imaginary, implicit conversations: between Machiavelli and his prince, Machiavelli and the reader, subjects and their rulers, princes and their advisers.[84] But in Machiavelli's view, words are less important than deeds; rhetoric is insignificant beside armed force.[85] His own writing is presented, not as a form of political activity, but as an inadequate substitute for it.[86] Machiavelli thus attacks the traditional hierarchy of values upheld by humanism. In place of ornate eloquence he offers simplicity; in place of learning, experience; in place of words, deeds; and in place of integrity, deception. All the literary techniques of the humanist are brought to bear, but one of the chief casualties is intended to be humanism itself.

It has, I think rightly, been argued that this is one of the reasons why Machiavelli seems to usher in the modern age.[87] But Machiavelli's claim to portray practical realities has provoked a number of postmodern readings.[88] Scholars have been eager to argue that his texts, like all other texts, fail to refer to anything outside themselves, that Machiavelli's arguments double back on themselves, his words shift their meaning, until in the end, the reader, far from being orientated, as by a map, is disorientated.[89] To use Machiavelli's works as a guide to how one should act is, on this view, as pointless as trying to step into a painting.

Machiavelli certainly wanted his texts to be somewhat enigmatic. Like Cesare Borgia's assassination of Remiro d'Orco, or Junius Brutus's execution of his sons, they were intended to seize the attention, and to juxtapose contraries (justice and cruelty, benevolence and hardness of heart) in enigmatic symbols whose meaning was both plain and difficult to render in words. I do not think, though, that Machiavelli would have taken kindly to the claim that his texts had no purchase on the world and offered no practical advice. He had worked for long years as a civil servant and was used to having his instructions obeyed, not dismissed as incomprehensible. *The Prince* is intended to be a guide to action, and to dismiss its references to reality as mere rhetoric is to dismiss it as a failure.

Nevertheless, Machiavelli was acutely conscious of the gap between theory and action, and well knew his own enterprise might be impractical. He addresses both *The Prince* and the *Discourses* to people he hopes will be in a position to put his theories into practice, but since his theories stressed the need to adapt action to circumstances, he could scarcely advise on how to implement them. Machiavelli looked to the past and to contemporary events to find examples to imitate, like a cook collecting recipes. But why should one expect what had worked on one occasion to work on another? Machiavelli stressed that if the political culture of a community had changed—if it had become corrupt, or virtuous—then strategies that had once failed would now work, and vice versa. Often two quite different approaches to a problem might be equally successful, so there was no need to imitate slavishly a successful strategy. Often the same policies, even when pursued in similar circumstances, might have different outcomes, for everything might depend on the politician's personal style, his ability to carry conviction. There was little point, then, in trying to persuade people to act contrary to their own natures, to play a part rather than be themselves, and yet what was Machiavelli doing but trying to persuade politicians to imitate others, and in the process forget themselves? Imitate the Romans, above all, and yet, as Machiavelli keeps pointing out, they had imitated no one, and followed no blueprint. In any case, Machiavelli insists, only a wise man can distinguish good advice from bad, and a wise man hardly needs advice in the first place. Following Machiavelli's advice turns out to be far from straightforward after all.[90]

"What a mistake some people make when they cite the Romans at every turn! One would need to be in a city like theirs before one could be justified in following their example."[91] So Machiavelli was criticized by his friend Guicciardini, and to such criticism he offers no straightforward reply. *The Prince* begins with a painting, an illusion of reality. The *Discourses* begins with fragments of Roman statues, dug out of the ground, passed around among scholars and imitated by artists. Imitating fragments does not enable you to reconstruct the shattered statues; new statues made in the style of the old are not Roman, but modern. Like the artists of his day, Machiavelli understands this perfectly well, but he still believes the secret of success lies in the imitation of the ancients. Guicciardini complained that people who imitated the Romans were like donkeys pretending to be race horses; Machiavelli, for his part, was impatient with people who lacked ambition and were prepared to make do with second best. To accept fortune, not struggle against her, might be prudent, but could scarcely be glorious.

If what most strikes readers of our generation is the slipperiness of the distinctions on which Machiavelli's argument depends—between Borgia and Agathocles, rhetoric and reality, imitation and self-expression—sixteenth- and seventeenth-century readers found him straightforward, even when teaching how to be deceptive. "We are much beholden to Machiavelli and other writers of that class who openly and unfeignedly declare or describe what men do, and not what they ought to do," said Bacon.[92] But to describe what men do was to teach immorality. "Murdrous Machiavel" Shakespeare called him. "Am I politic, am I subtle, am I Machiavel?" one of his characters asks.[93] Since Machiavelli's works were placed on the Index in 1559, his name has been associated with evil. Yet few authors have been more widely read, more commented upon, and, indeed, have provoked such strong loyalty and admiration.

As soon as we begin to approach the study of Machiavelli we find ourselves facing a series of conflicting images out of which it is very difficult to resolve a coherent picture of a man or a consistent doctrine. In *The Prince* Machiavelli seems to advocate tyranny; yet in the *Discourses* he praises freedom. Even within these works we find in close combination arguments we would expect to be irreconcilable. In order to maximize his own power, the prince, it turns out, must serve the interests of his subjects. In order to build freedom, a society must conquer and enslave others. Machiavelli looks forward: He declares he has discovered a new continent of knowledge, and some think modernity begins with him. But at the same time he looks backward: His only recommendation is that we imitate the Romans, and some think he is best understood as reviving Roman values. Some, like Bacon, see him as the founder of a new, objective science of politics, concerned not with what should be, but with what is, not with hopes and fears, but with practical realities. Others insist he is an idealist, constantly striving for justice, freedom, and equality. Some believe he is a cynic, while others claim he is a moralist. He is, it seems, simultaneously open and unfeigning, yet politic and subtle.

When it comes to Machiavelli, every reader has to make up her or his own mind on how to reconcile the irreconcilable. In this introduction I have tried to outline the main orthodoxies that are entrenched in current scholarship, while pointing out a number of alternative views, some of which seem to me persuasive. Would Machiavelli have recognized himself in my portrait of him? He would at least have been gratified at the thought that we might sit down to discuss politics with him, as he discussed politics with Livy.

In the translations that follow, I have done my best to let him speak in his own voice. Others before me have produced translations that, taken word by word, are closer to Machiavelli's text. My primary concern has been to convey the sense and the style, which is aphoristic, lively, persuasive. Machiavelli was never the dull, worthy, pedantic author who appears in the pages of other translations.[94] But it is time to stop speaking about him, for I have done my best to let him speak for himself.

Notes

1. Roberto Ridolfi, *The Life of Niccolò Machiavelli*, trans. C. Grayson (Chicago: University of Chicago Press, 1963), 133–38; Sebastian de Grazia, *Machiavelli in Hell* (Princeton, N.J.: Princeton University Press, 1989), 32–40; C. H. Clough, *Machiavelli Researches* (Naples: Publicazioni della Sezione romanza dell'Istituto universitario orientale, 1967), 33.

2. John H. Langbein, *Torture and the Law of Proof* (Chicago: University of Chicago Press, 1977).

3. E.g., Vettori to Machiavelli, 23 November 1513; Machiavelli to Vettori, 19 December 1513; Francesco Guicciardini to Machiavelli, 17 May 1521: Niccolò Machiavelli, *Lettere*, ed. F. Gaeta (Milan: Feltrinelli, 1961) [*Opere*, vol. 6], 298, 308–9, 401–2.

4. Elizabeth L. Eisenstein, *The Printing Revolution in Early Modern Europe* (Cambridge: Cambridge University Press, 1983).

5. S. Bertelli, "Noterelle Machiavelliane," *Rivista storica italiana* 73 (1961), 544–53. In his lifetime, Machiavelli published an amusing play, *Mandragola*, and a poem, the *Decennale primo*, but only one book in which he displayed his

professional skills: *The Art of War* (1521). Copies of his *The Prince* circulated in manuscript, and it was published only after his death.

6. Carlo M. Cipolla, *European Culture and Overseas Expansion* (Harmondsworth: Penguin Books, 1970), 38.

7. Arnaldo Momigliano, "Polybius' Reappearance in Western Europe," [1973] in his *Sesto contributo alla storia degli studi classici e del mondo antico* (2 vols., Rome: Edizioni di storia e letteratura, 1980), 103–23, at 114–15.

8. Nicolai Rubinstein, "Machiavelli and the World of Florentine Politics," in *Studies on Machiavelli*, ed. M. P. Gilmore (Florence: Sansoni, 1972), 5–28, at 7. Ridolfi, however, does not find the evidence convincing: *Life of Niccolò Machiavelli*, 257, n. 4.

9. Machiavelli to Guicciardini, 3 January 1526: "Always, as far back as I can remember, war has either been going on or has been talked about. . . ." *Opere*, 6:451; for a translation, see Niccolò Machiavelli, *The Chief Works and Others*, ed. and trans. Allan Gilbert (3 vols., Durham, N.C.: Duke University Press, 1965), 2:991.

10. Quoted in Garrett Mattingly, *Renaissance Diplomacy* [1955] (Harmondsworth: Penguin Books, 1965), 111.

11. Machiavelli, *Chief Works*, 2:895–97. This letter was once thought to have been written to Soderini shortly after his fall, but is now known to have been written as early as 1506, not to Piero Soderini but to his nephew, Giovan Battista: R. Ridolfi and P. Ghiglieri, "I *ghiribizzi* al Soderini," *La bibliofilia* 72 (1970), 53–74; M. Martelli, " 'I ghiribizzi' a Giovan Battista Soderini," *Rinascimento* 9 (1969), 147–80.

12. Carlo Dionisotti, "Machiavelli, Cesare Borgia e don Micheletto" [1967], in his *Machiavellerie* (Turin: Einaudi, 1980), 3–59. See Roslyn Pesman Cooper, "Machiavelli, Francesco Soderini and Don Michelotto," *Nuova rivista storica* 66 (1982), 342–57, and Robert Black, "Machiavelli, Servant of the Florentine Republic," in *Machiavelli and Republicanism*, ed. G. Bock, Q. Skinner, and M. Viroli (Cambridge: Cambridge University Press, 1990), 71–99.

13. Felix Gilbert, "Machiavelli: the Renaissance of the Art of War," in *Makers of Modern Strategy: From Machiavelli to the Nuclear Age*, ed. P. Paret (Princeton, N.J.: Princeton University Press, 1986), 11–31.

14. *Discourses*, bk. 3, ch. 3.

15. Machiavelli, *Chief Works*, 3:1463.

16. John M. Najemy, "The Controversy Surrounding Machiavelli's Service to the Republic," in *Machiavelli and Republicanism*, ed. Bock et al., 101–17.

17. Note Machiavelli's insistence in 1520 that Florence needed to have someone in charge: Niccolò Machiavelli, *Arte della guerra e scritti politici minori*, ed. S. Bertelli (Milan: Feltrinelli, 1961) [*Opere*, vol. 2], 265; *Chief Works*, 1:105; and the views attributed to him in 1512 by Giovanni Folchi: J. N. Stephens and H. C. Butters, "New Light on Machiavelli," *English Historical Review* 97 (1982), 54–69, at 67.

18. E.g. Q. Skinner, *Machiavelli* (Oxford: Oxford University Press, 1981), 24; idem, "Introduction" to N. Machiavelli, *The Prince*, ed. Q. Skinner and R. Price (Cambridge: Cambridge University Press, 1988), ix–xxiv, at xii–xiii.

19. The arguments involved are important, even if, in my view, wrong. See Garrett Mattingly, "Machiavelli's *Prince*: Political Science or Political Satire?" *American Scholar* 27 (1958), 482–91; Mary G. Dietz, "Trapping the Prince: Machiavelli and the Politics of Deception," *American Political Science Review* 80 (1986), 777–99; Stephen M. Fallon, "Hunting the Fox: Equivocation and Authorial Duplicity in *The Prince*," *PMLA* 107 (1992), 1181–95. On Machiavelli's attitude to deception, Wayne Rebhorn, *Foxes and Lions: Machiavelli's Confidence Men* (Ithaca: Cornell University Press, 1988). One of the merits of the Mattingly approach is that it is an interpretation that would have amused Machiavelli. Moreover, it would seem reasonable to argue that Machiavelli did not intend intelligent readers to take everything he says in *The Prince* literally: One is bound to suspect the religious language of the last chapter is, at least in part, a joke.

20. Clough, *Machiavelli Researches*, 27–79. Much of the evidence supporting this view is brought to the fore in Hans Baron's essays (below, n. 48), but he seems to have been unwilling to commit himself to it: See his review of Clough in *English Historical Review* 84 (1969), 579–82. For criticism of an earlier version of Clough's argument, see Gennaro Sasso, "Filosofia o 'scopo pratico' nel *Principe*?" in his *Studi su Machiavelli* (Naples: Morano, 1967), 81–110. For a differing view, which I find unconvincing, J. N. Stephens, "Machiavelli's *Prince* and the Florentine Revolution of 1512," *Italian Studies* 41 (1986), 45–61.

21. For the exception, see below, p. 65. Petrucci, like the Medici, was trying to hold on to power in a city used to political freedom.

22. J. J. Marchand, *Niccolò Machiavelli, i primi scritti politici (1499–1512)* (Padua: Antenore, 1975), 533–35; *Chief Works*, 1:101–15; *Opere*, 2:261–77.

23. Machiavelli, *Opere*, 6:331; *Chief Works*, 2:926–27. The date of this letter is uncertain. Redating it to September, as proposed in John M. Najemy, *Between Friends* (Princeton, N.J.: Princeton University Press, 1993), 277–78, would not significantly affect the argument.

24. J.G.A. Pocock, *The Machiavellian Moment: Florentine Political Thought and the Atlantic Republican Tradition* (Princeton, N.J.: Princeton University Press, 1975), 160.

25. See below, p. 4. Also Machiavelli to Vettori, 16 April 1513: *Opere*, 6:244; *Chief Works*, 2:902. Machiavelli expected Giuliano to assist him because they had an association that predated the fall of the Medici in 1494: M. Martelli, "Preistoria (medicea) di Machiavelli," *Studi di filologia italiana* 29 (1971), 377–405.

26. Vettori to Machiavelli, 24 December 1513: *Opere*, 6:312.

27. See the half dozen letters between Machiavelli and Vettori in December 1514: *Opere*, 6:348–70.

28. As Machiavelli himself feared: Second letter to Vettori, 20 December 1514: *Opere*, 6:366; *Chief Works*, 2:958.

29. See Vettori to Machiavelli, 12 July 1513: *Opere*, 6:267–70. In my view, this was in all probability the immediate inspiration of *The Prince*. Also Vettori to Machiavelli, 16 May 1514 (idem, 336–37).

30. Machiavelli to Vettori, 31 January 1515: *Opere*, 6:374–75; *Chief Works*, 2:962–63. I am not, I think, persuaded by the intriguing interpretation of the letter proposed by Najemy, *Between Friends*, 333–34. Machiavelli's appointment was vetoed by Cardinal Giulio de' Medici: Hans Baron, "The *Principe* and the Puzzle of the Date of Chapter Twenty-Six," *Journal of Medieval and Renaissance Studies* 21 (1991), 83–102, at 99.

31. As Vettori put it, 12 July 1513: "Non voglio entrare in consideratione quale stato disegni, perché in questo muterà proposito, secondo la occasione." Machiavelli, *Opere*, 6:268–69.

32. Baron, "The *Principe* and the Puzzle of the Date of Chapter Twenty-Six." For a discussion of Mario Martelli's view that chapter twenty-six was written in 1518 ("Da Poliziano a Machiavelli: sull'epigramma *dell'occasione* e sull'occasione," *Interpres* 2 (1979), 230–54), see Najemy, *Between Friends*, 177–85. I am persuaded by several of his arguments against Martelli, but by none of those against Baron.

33. Hans Baron, "Machiavelli the Republican Citizen and Author of *The Prince*" [1961], in his *In Search of Florentine Civic Humanism* (2 vols., Princeton, N.J.: Princeton University Press, 1988), 2:101–51, at 130–31.

34. Cf. Vettori to Machiavelli, 12 July 1513: *Opere*, 6:268.

35. R. Pesman Cooper, "Machiavelli, Pier Soderini and *Il Principe*," in *Altro Polo: A Volume of Italian Renaissance Studies*, ed. C. Condren and R. Pesman Cooper (Sydney: Fredrick May Foundation, University of Sydney, 1982), 119–44.

36. Cf. Machiavelli to Vettori, 31 January 1515: *Opere*, 6:375; *Chief Works*, 2:962.

37. *Discourses*, bk. 1, ch. 26.

38. Victoria Kahn, "*Virtù* and the example of Agathocles in Machiavelli's *Prince*," [1986] in *Machiavelli and the Discourse of Literature*, ed. A. R. Ascoli and V. Kahn (Iathaca: Cornell University Press, 1993), 195–217.

39. *Discourses*, bk. 1, ch. 10.

40. Machiavelli, *Opere*, 2:268; *Chief Works*, 1:107.

41. E.g. *Discourses*, bk. 3, ch. 40.

42. Cf. *Discourses*, bk. 1, ch. 9; bk. 3, ch. 41. In chapter eighteen of *The Prince* it is the common man, not Machiavelli, who always approves of success.

43. The first sentence of chapter eight of *The Prince* is sometimes taken to be a reference to the *Discourses* (e.g., surprisingly, Baron, "Machiavelli: Citizen and Author," 112), though it seems evident to me it is a reference to chapter nine.

44. J. H. Whitfield, *Machiavelli* (Oxford: Blackwell, 1947).

45. John Plamenatz, "In Search of Machiavellian *virtù*," in *The Political Calculus*, ed. A. Parel (Toronto: University of Toronto Press, 1972), 157–78.

46. Federico Chabod, *Machiavelli and the Renaissance* (New York: Harper and Row, 1965).

47. Mark Hulliung, *Citizen Machiavelli* (Princeton, N.J.: Princeton University Press, 1983).

48. Hans Baron, "The *Principe* and the Puzzle of the Date of the *Discorsi*," *Bibliothèque d'Humanisme et Renaissance* 18 (1956), 405–28; idem, "Machiavelli the Republican Citizen and Author of *The Prince*"; idem, "The *Principe* and the Puzzle of the Date of Chapter Twenty-Six."

49. There has been a good deal of discussion about when the *Discourses* were written and how Machiavelli's project may have changed over time. The most influential account is Felix Gilbert, "The Composition and Structure of Machiavelli's *Discorsi*" [1953], in his *History: Choice and Commitment* (Cambridge, Mass.: Harvard University Press, 1977), 115–33; most recent is F. Bausi, *I "Discorsi" di Niccolò Machiavelli. Genesi e strutture* (Florence: Sansoni, 1985).

50. In *Discourses*, bk. 1, ch. 55, Machiavelli insists it would be impossible to establish a republic in either Naples or the Romagna.

51. I owe this point to R. F. Tannenbaum.

52. Machiavelli, *Chief Works*, 2:1015. Also on thrush-hunting, see the letter to Vettori of 25 February 1514: *Opere*, 6: 327–30; *Chief Works*, 2:938–41.

53. Machiavelli, *Opere*, 6:239; *Chief Works*, 2:900.

54. *Discourses*, bk. 1, ch. 10.

55. See Machiavelli's correspondence between April and November 1520: *Opere*, 6:386–97.

56. Louis Green, "Machiavelli's *Vita di Castruccio Castracani* and its Lucchese Model," *Italian Studies* 42 (1987), 37–55.

57. Cf. below pp. 71–72.

58. Niccolò Machiavelli, *Istorie fiorentine*, ed. F. Gaeta (Milan: Feltrinelli, 1962) [*Opere*, vol. 7], 36; *Chief Works*, 2:555.

59. Felix Gilbert, "Machiavelli's *Istorie fiorentine*," in his *History: Choice and Commitment*, 135–53, at 142–43.

60. E.g. Leo Strauss, *Thoughts on Machiavelli* (Glencoe, Ill.: The Free Press, 1958); Harvey C. Mansfield, *Machiavelli's New Modes and Orders: A Study of the "Discourses on Livy"* (Ithaca: Cornell University Press, 1979).

61. Russell Price, "Self-Love, 'Egoism' and *ambizione* in Machiavelli's Thought," *History of Political Thought* 9 (1988), 237–61.

62. Maurizio Viroli, "Machiavelli and the Republican Conception of Politics," in his *From Politics to Reason of State* (Cambridge: Cambridge University Press, 1992), 126–77. It would suit my own argument to stress, as Viroli does, "the

absence of any *politico*-rooted word in *The Prince*" (128), but it would be wrong to make too much of this as, for Machiavelli, *civile* is a synonym for *politico*.

63. Marcia L. Colish, "Cicero's *De officiis* and Machiavelli's *Prince*," *Sixteenth Century Journal* 9 (1978), 81–93.

64. John Freccero, "Medusa and the Madonna of Forlì: Political Sexuality in Machiavelli," in *Machiavelli and the Discourse of Literature*, ed. Ascoli and Kahn, 161–78, at 163–64.

65. A mistake, I should say, that the standard discussions do not make. See Hannah Pitkin, *Fortune is a Woman* (Berkeley, Cal.: University of California Press, 1984), and Wendy Brown, *Manhood and Politics* (Totowa, N.J.: Rowman and Littlefield, 1988), 71–123. On Renaissance views on gender, Ian Maclean, *The Renaissance Notion of Woman* (Cambridge: Cambridge University Press, 1980) and Constance Jordan, *Renaissance Feminism* (Ithaca: Cornell University Press, 1990) are helpful.

66. Giulio Ferroni, " 'Transformation' and 'Adaptation' in Machiavelli's *Mandragola*" [1972], in *Machiavelli and the Discourse of Literature*, ed. Ascoli and Kahn, 81–116, at 99.

67. Ronald L. Martinez, "Benefit of Absence: Machiavellian Valediction in *Clizia*," in *Machiavelli and the Discourse of Literature*, ed. Ascoli and Kahn, 117–44, at 139.

68. Freccero, "Medusa and the Madonna." Machiavelli even uses for the countess's genital organs a term usually used only for men (175–76).

69. Sheldon S. Wolin, *Politics and Vision* (Boston: Little, Brown, 1960), 220–24.

70. For fine analyses of Machiavelli's deliberate cultivation of contrasting attitudes, styles, and tones of voice see Ferroni, " 'Transformation' and 'Adaptation'," and idem, "Le 'cose vane' nelle *Lettere* di Machiavelli," *La rassegna della letteratura italiana* 76 (1972), 215–64.

71. Nicola Matteucci: "Il *vivere libero* . . . è usato esclusivamente per le repubbliche," "Machiavelli Politologo," in *Studies on Machiavelli*, ed. Gilmore, 209–48, at 222. Contrast Baron, "Machiavelli: Citizen and Author," 114. A helpful context for Machiavelli's views on liberty is provided by Patricia J. Osmond, "Sallust and Machiavelli: From Civic Humanism to Political Prudence," *Journal of Medieval and Renaissance Studies* 23 (1993), 407–38.

72. Quentin Skinner, "The Republican Ideal of Political Liberty," in *Machiavelli and Republicanism*, ed. Bock et al., 293–309, at 301–6, seems to me to provide an idealistic reading of Machiavelli, employing phrases such as "willingly to serve the common good" and "devote ourselves wholeheartedly to a life of public service." Compare his earlier discussion of the same question, *Machiavelli*, 64–67: "Although motivated entirely by their selfish interests, the factions will thus be guided, as if by an invisible hand, to promote the public interest. . . . "

73. John M. Najemy, "*Arti* and *ordini* in Machiavelli's *Istorie fiorentine*," in *Essays Presented to Myron Gilmore*, ed. S. Bertelli and G. Ramakus (Florence:

La nuova italia, 1978), 161–91. Mark Phillips, "Barefoot Boy Makes Good: A Study of Machiavelli's Historiography," *Speculum* 59 (1984), 585–605.

74. See Gisela Bock, "Civil Discord in Machiavelli's *Istorie fiorentine*," in *Machiavelli and Republicanism*, ed. Bock et al, 181–202.

75. Machiavelli does consider the possibility of a federation of cities, such as that of the ancient Tuscans, but the problem is only postponed: The freedom of such a federation depends on its conquering its neighbors.

76. See the excellent translation of the tercets "On Ambition" in de Grazia, *Machiavelli in Hell*, 165–66.

77. I am grateful to Matthew Carrington for discussing this question with me.

78. Michael Baxandall, *Painting and Experience in Fifteenth-Century Italy* (Oxford: Oxford University Press, 1972), 14–23.

79. Ludwig H. Heydenreich, "The Military Architect," in *Leonardo the Inventor*, ed. L. W. Heydenreich, B. Dibner, L. Reti (New York: McGraw-Hill, 1980), 11–71.

80. Machiavelli, *Opere*, 7:303–4; *Chief Works*, 3:1214. In *Discourses* bk. 1, ch. 1 he also mentions Deinocrates, a civil engineer like Brunelleschi, Leonardo, and Machiavelli himself.

81. Characteristically, in chapter fourteen of *The Prince*, he claims that Scipio imitated Cyrus, not that those writing about Scipio have imitated Xenophon.

82. Quentin Skinner, "Thomas Hobbes: Rhetoric and the Construction of Morality," *Proceedings of the British Academy* 76 (1990), 1–61, at 23–25.

83. Cf. Machiavelli, *Opere*, 2:518; *Chief Works*, 2:724.

84. Salvatore di Maria, "La struttura dialogica nel *Principe* di Machiavelli," *MLN* 99 (1984), 65–79.

85. Quentin Skinner, *The Foundations of Modern Political Thought* (2 vols., Cambridge: Cambridge University Press, 1978), 1:129–31.

86. A. R. Ascoli and V. Kahn, "Introduction" to *Machiavelli and the Discourse of Literature*, ed. Ascoli and Kahn, 1–15.

87. Robert Hariman, "Composing Modernity in Machiavelli's Prince" [1989], in *Renaissance Essays II*, ed. W. J. Connell (Rochester, N.Y.: University of Rochester Press, 1993), 224–50.

88. E.g. Eugene M. Garver, "Machiavelli's *The Prince*: A Neglected Rhetorical Classic," *Philosophy and Rhetoric* 13 (1980), 99–120; Michael McCanles, *The Discourse of "Il principe"* (Malibu: Undena, 1983); Thomas M. Greene, "The End of Discourse in Machiavelli's *Prince*," *Yale French Studies* 67 (1984), 57–71; Barbara Spackman, "Machiavelli and Maxims," *Yale French Studies* 77 (1990), 137–55; idem, "Politics on the Warpath: Machiavelli's *Art of War*," in *Machiavelli and the Discourse of Literature*, ed. Ascoli and Kahn, 179–93; Jeffrey T. Schnapp, "Machiavellian Foundlings: Castruccio Castracani and the Aphorism," *Renaissance Quarterly* 45 (1992), 653–76.

89. Machiavelli's own interest in diagrams is relevant: J. R. Hale, "A Humanistic Visual Aid. The Military Diagram in the Renaissance," *Renaissance Studies*

2 (1988), 281–98, stresses the novelty of the diagrams accompanying the *Art of War*.

90. John D. Lyons, "Machiavelli: Example and Origin," in his *Exemplum: the Rhetoric of Example in Early Modern France and Italy* (Princeton, N.J.: Princeton University Press, 1989), 35–71; Timothy Hampton, *Writing from History: The Rhetoric of Exemplarity in Renaissance Literature* (Ithaca, N.Y.: Cornell University Press, 1990), 62–79.

91. Francesco Guicciardini, *Ricordi*, ed. R. Spongano (Florence: Sansoni, 1951), 110; idem, *Maxims and Reflections of a Renaissance Statesman* (New York: Harper and Row, 1965), 69.

92. Francis Bacon, *Works*, ed. J. Spedding, R. L. Ellis, D. D. Heath (15 vols., Cambridge, Mass.: Riverside Press, 1863), 3:31; 6:327.

93. Shakespeare, *3 Henry 6*, 3.02.193; *Merry Wives of Windsor*, 3.01.101.

94. Nietzsche defined what a good translation would be like when he wrote: "But how could the German language, even in the prose of a Lessing, imitate the tempo of Machiavelli, who in his *Principe* lets us breathe the subtle dry air of Florence and cannot help presenting the most serious affairs in a boisterous *allegrissimo*: not perhaps without a malicious artist's sense of the contrast he is risking—thoughts protracted, difficult, hard, dangerous and the tempo of the gallop and the most wanton good humour." Friedrich Nietzsche, *Beyond Good and Evil*, trans. R. J. Hollingdale (Harmondsworth: Penguin Books, 1973), 41–42.

FURTHER READING

The standard edition of Machiavelli's *The Prince* and *Discourses* is that edited by S. Bertelli as vol. 1 of Niccolò Machiavelli, *Opere* ed. S. Bertelli and F. Gaeta (8 vols., Milan: Feltrinelli, 1960–65). I have followed this edition throughout, with the single exception of the penultimate sentence of chapter eighteen of *The Prince*, where I have followed the alternate reading of the Gotha manuscript. Although for convenience I have cited the edition of the letters in the same series, a better edition now is that edited by F. Gaeta (Turin: UTET, 1984). The most extensive selection of Machiavelli's works in English is *Chief Works, and Others*, ed. and trans. A. Gilbert (3 vols., Durham, N.C.: Duke University Press, 1965).

The best short introduction to Machiavelli's thought is Quentin Skinner, *Machiavelli* (Oxford: Oxford University Press, 1981). Two useful collections of articles are *Machiavelli and Republicanism*, ed. G. Bock, Q. Skinner and M. Viroli (Cambridge: Cambridge University Press, 1990) and *Machiavelli and the Discourse of Literature*, ed. A. R. Ascoli and V. Kahn (Ithaca: Cornell University Press, 1993). A valuable study of Machiavelli's life is Sebastian de Grazia, *Machiavelli in Hell* (Princeton, N.J.: Princeton University Press, 1989), although his account of Machiavelli's attitude to Christianity is unconvincing: Compare Alberto Tenenti, "La religione di Machiavelli," *Studi storici* 10 (1969), 709–48.

Two articles on Machiavelli are of outstanding importance: Hans Baron, "Machiavelli the Republican Citizen and Author of *The Prince*" [1961], rev. ed. in H. Baron, *In Search of Florentine Civic Humanism* (2 vols., Princeton, N.J.: Princeton University Press, 1988), 2:101–51, and Isaiah Berlin, "The Originality of Machiavelli," in *Studies on Machiavelli*, ed. M. P. Gilmore (Florence: Sansoni, 1972), 149–206. For a close reading of a famous text one may single out the discussion of the letter to Vettori of 10 December 1513 in John M. Najemy, "Machiavelli and Geta: Men of Letters," *Machiavelli and the Discourse of Literature*, ed. Ascoli and Kahn, 53–79.

Six essays on Machiavelli's vocabulary provide introductions to the key terms: Russell Price, "The Senses of *virtù* in Machiavelli," *European Studies Review* 3 (1973), 315–45; J. H. Hexter, "*Il principe* and *lo stato*" [1957], in *The Vision of Politics on the Eve of the Reformation* (London:

(London: Allen Lane, 1973), 150–78; J. H. Whitfield, "On Machiavelli's Use of *ordini*" [1955], in his *Discourses on Machiavelli* (Cambridge: W. Heffer and Sons, 1969), 141–62, and "The Politics of Machiavelli," idem, 163–79; M. Colish, "The Idea of Liberty in Machiavelli" [1971], in *Renaissance Essays II*, ed. W. J. Connell (Rochester, N.Y.: University of Rochester Press, 1993), 180–207; Hannah Pitkin, "Fortune," in her *Fortune is a Woman* (Berkeley, Cal.: University of California Press, 1984), chapter six.

A recent study of the wider context of Machiavelli's political thought is Maurizio Viroli, *From Politics to Reason of State* (Cambridge: Cambridge University Press, 1992). For Florentine politics in Machiavelli's lifetime, H. C. Butters, *Governors and Government in Early Sixteenth-Century Florence, 1502–1519* (Oxford: Clarendon Press, 1985). For a survey of Machiavelli's influence, see Felix Gilbert, "Machiavellism" [1973], in his *History: Choice and Commitment* (Cambridge, Mass.: Harvard University Press, 1977), 155–76. Finally, the vast body of scholarship on Machiavelli that appeared between 1935 and 1985 is surveyed in Silvia R. Fiore, *Niccolò Machiavelli: An Annotated Bibliography of Modern Criticism and Scholarship* (Westport, Conn.: Greenwood, 1990).

Acknowledgments: I would like to thank William Connell, Alan Houston, Donald Kelley, John Najemy, Quentin Skinner, Robert Tannenbaum, Maurizio Viroli, and Blair Worden for their comments on a draft of the Introduction, and Jack Hexter and Paul Spade for their comments on sections of the translation. Kindness takes many forms, and criticizing a colleague's sloppy thinking and bad grammar is one of them. Matthew Carrington, John Kavcic, and Lesley Sutton have taught me more than I have taught them. The errors that remain are mine alone.

LETTER TO FRANCESCO VETTORI

To His Excellency the Florentine Ambassador to his Holiness the Pope, and my benefactor, Francesco Vettori, in Rome.

Your Excellency. "Favors from on high are always timely, never late."[1] I say this because I had begun to think I had, if not lost, then mislaid your goodwill, for you had allowed so long to go by without writing to me, and I was in some uncertainty as to what the reason could be. All the explanations I could think of seemed to me worthless, except for the possibility that occurred to me, that you might have stopped writing to me because someone had written to tell you I was not taking proper care of your letters to me; but I knew that I had not been responsible for their being shown to anyone else, with the exception of Filippo and Paolo.[2]

Anyway, I have now received your most recent letter of the 23rd of last month. I was delighted to learn you are fulfilling your official responsibilities without fussing and flapping. I encourage you to carry on like this, for anyone who sacrifices his own convenience in order to make others happy is bound to inconvenience himself, but can't be sure of receiving any thanks for it. And since fortune wants to control everything, she evidently wants to be left a free hand; meanwhile we should keep our own counsel and not get in her way, and wait until she allows human beings to have a say in the course of events. That will be the time for you to work harder, and keep a closer eye on events, and for me to leave my country house and say: "Here I am!"

Since I want to repay your kind gesture, I have no alternative but to describe to you in this letter of mine how I live my life. If you decide you'd like to swap my life for yours, I'll be happy to make a deal.

I am still in my country house. Since my recent difficulties began I have not been, adding them all together, more than twenty days in Florence. Until recently I have been setting bird snares with my own hands. I've been getting up before dawn, making the bird-lime, and setting out with a bundle of cages on my back, so I look like Geta

1. Petrarch, *Trionfo della Divinità*, 13.

2. Paolo is Francesco Vettori's brother; Filippo Casavecchia was a close mutual friend.

when he comes back from the harbor laden down with Amphitryo's books.[3] I always caught at least two thrushes, but never more than six. This is how I spent September;[4] since then I am sorry to say I have had to give up my rather nasty and peculiar hobby, so I will describe the life I lead now.

I get up in the morning at daybreak and go to a wood of mine where I am having some timber felled. I stay there two hours to check on the work done during the preceding day and to chat to the woodcutters, who are always involved in some conflict, either among themselves or with the neighbors. I could tell you a thousand fine stories about my dealings over this wood, both with Frosino da Panzano and with others who wanted some of the timber. Frosino in particular had them supply some cords without mentioning it to me, and when I asked for payment he wanted to knock off ten lire he said I had owed him for four years, ever since he beat me at cards at Antonio Guicciardini's. I began to cut up rough; I threatened to charge with theft the wagon driver who had fetched the wood. However, Giovanni Machiavelli intervened, and got us to settle our differences. Batista Guicciardini, Filippo Ginori, Tommaso del Bene, and a number of other citizens each bought a cord from me when the cold winds were blowing. I made promises to all of them, and supplied one to Tommaso. But in Florence it turned out to be only half a cord, because there were he, his wife, his servants, and his sons to stack it: They looked like Gabburra on a Thursday when, assisted by his workmen, he slaughters an ox.[5] Then, realizing I wasn't the one who was getting a good deal, I told the others I had run out of wood. They've all complained bitterly about it; especially Battista, who thinks this is as bad as anything else that has happened as a result of the battle of Prato.[6]

When I leave the wood I go to a spring, and from there to check my bird-nets. I carry a book with me: Dante, or Petrarch, or one of the minor poets, perhaps Tibullus, Ovid, or someone like that. I read about their infatuations and their love affairs, reminisce about my own,

3. See John M. Najemy, "Machiavelli and Geta: Men of Letters," in *Machiavelli and the Discourse of Literature*, ed. Ascoli and Kahn, 53–79.

4. Ridolfi points out that Machiavelli must have meant to write November, since this is the month for thrush hunting.

5. In other words, just as the butcher turns a large ox into a small pile of steaks, so Tommaso and his family turned a large pile of wood into a small, neat, and cheap stack.

6. The Battle of Prato (1512) had led to the downfall of Soderini, the return of the Medici, and Machiavelli's own dismissal from office.

and enjoy my reveries for a while. Then I set out on the road to the inn. I chat to those who pass by, asking them for news about the places they come from. I pick up bits and pieces of information, and study the differing tastes and various preoccupations of mankind. It's lunchtime before I know it. I sit down with my family to eat such food as I can grow on my wretched farm or pay for with the income from my tiny inheritance. Once I have eaten I go back to the inn. The landlord will be there, and, usually, the butcher, the miller, and a couple of kiln owners. With them I muck about all day, playing card games. We get into endless arguments and are constantly calling each other names. Usually we only wager a quarter, and yet you could hear us shouting if you were in San Casciano. So, in the company of these bumpkins, I keep my brain from turning moldy, and put up with the hostility fate has shown me. I am happy for fate to see to what depths I have sunk, for I want to know if she will be ashamed of herself for what she has done.

When evening comes, I go back home, and go to my study. On the threshold I take off my work clothes, covered in mud and filth, and put on the clothes an ambassador would wear. Decently dressed, I enter the ancient courts of rulers who have long since died. There I am warmly welcomed, and I feed on the only food I find nourishing, and was born to savor. I am not ashamed to talk to them, and to ask them to explain their actions. And they, out of kindness, answer me. Four hours go by without my feeling any anxiety. I forget every worry. I am no longer afraid of poverty, or frightened of death. I live entirely through them.

And because Dante says there is no point in studying unless you remember what you have learned, I have made notes of what seem to me the most important things I have learned in my dialogue with the dead, and written a little book *On princedoms*[7] in which I go as deeply as I can into the questions relevant to my subject. I discuss what a principality is, how many types of principality there are, how one acquires them, how one holds onto them, why one loses them. And if any of my little productions have ever pleased you, then this one ought not to displease you; and a ruler, especially a new ruler, ought to be delighted by it. Consequently, I have addressed it to His Highness Giuliano.[8] Filippo Casavecchia has seen it; he can give you a preliminary report, both on the text, and on the discussions I have had with him: though I am still adding to the text and polishing it.

7. *De principatibus*, Machiavelli calls it.
8. Giuliano de' Medici, the senior member of the Medici family after his brother, Pope Leo X.

You may well wish, Your Excellency, that I should give up this life, and come and enjoy yours with you. I will do so if I can; what holds me back at the moment is some business that won't take me more than six weeks to finish. Though I am a bit concerned the Soderini family is there,[9] and I will be obliged, if I come, to visit them and socialize with them. My concern is that I might intend my return journey to end at my own house, but find myself instead dismounting at the prison gates. For although this government is well established and solidly based, still it is new, and consequently suspicious, nor is there a shortage of clever fellows who, in order to get a reputation like Pagolo Bertini's, would put me in prison, and leave me to worry about how to get out. I beg you to persuade me this fear is irrational, and then I will make every effort to come and visit you before six weeks are up.

I have discussed my little book with Filippo, asking him whether it was a good idea to present it or not; and if I ought to present it, then whether I should deliver it in person, or whether I should send it through you. My concern is that if I do not deliver it in person Giuliano may not read it; even worse, that chap Ardinghelli[10] may claim the credit for my latest effort. In favor of presenting it is the fact that the wolf is at the door, for my funds are running down, and I cannot continue like this much longer without becoming so poor I lose face. In any case, I would like their lordships, the Medici, to start putting me to use, even if they only assign me some menial task, for if, once I was in their employment, I did not win their favor, I would have only myself to blame. As for my book, if they were to read it, they would see the fifteen years I have spent studying statecraft have not been wasted: I haven't been asleep at my desk or playing cards. Anyone should be keen to employ someone who has had plenty of experience and has learned from the mistakes he made at his previous employers' expense. As for my integrity, nobody should question it: For I have always kept my word, and I am not going to start breaking it now. Someone who has been honest and true for forty-three years, as I have been, isn't going to be able to change character. And that I am honest and true is evident from my poverty.

So: I would like you to write to me again and let me have your opinion on this matter. I give you my regards. Best wishes.

Niccolò Machiavegli in Florence

10 December 1513.

9. Piero and his brother Cardinal Francesco were in Rome.
10. Secretary to Pope Leo X.

THE PRINCE[1]

Niccolò Machiavelli to His Magnificence Lorenzo de' Medici[2]

Those who wish to acquire favor with a ruler most often approach him with those among their possessions that are most valuable in their eyes, or that they are confident will give him pleasure. So rulers are often given horses, armor, cloth of gold, precious stones, and similar ornaments that are thought worthy of their social eminence. Since I want to offer myself to your Magnificence, along with something that will symbolize my desire to give you obedient service, I have found nothing among my possessions I value more, or would put a higher price upon, than an understanding of the deeds of great men, acquired through a lengthy experience of contemporary politics and through an uninterrupted study of the classics. Since I have long thought about and studied the question of what makes for greatness, and have now summarized my conclusions on the subject in a little book, it is this I send your Magnificence.

And although I recognize this book is unworthy to be given to Yourself, yet I trust that out of kindness you will accept it, taking account of the fact there is no greater gift I can present to you than the opportunity to understand, after a few hours of reading, everything I have learned over the course of so many years, and have undergone so many discomforts and dangers to discover. I have not ornamented this book with rhetorical turns of phrase, or stuffed it with pretentious and magnificent words, or made use of allurements and embellishments that are irrelevant to my purpose, as many authors do. For my intention has been that my book should be without pretensions, and should rely

1. For an edition of *The Prince* which provides extensive notes and apparatus see *Il Principe*, ed. L. Arthur Burd (Oxford: Clarendon Press, 1891, repr. 1968): The text is in Italian, but the notes and apparatus are in English.

2. Lorenzo (1492–1519) was the grandson of Lorenzo the Magnificent (1449–92), son of Piero de' Medici (1471–1503, ruler of Florence, 1492–94), and nephew of Giovanni de' Medici (1475–1521), who became Pope Leo X in 1513. Lorenzo became Duke of Urbino in 1516. We know Machiavelli originally intended to give *The Prince* to Lorenzo's uncle and Leo's brother, Giuliano de' Medici (1479–1516).

entirely on the variety of the examples and the importance of the subject to win approval.

I hope it will not be thought presumptuous for someone of humble and lowly status to dare to discuss the behavior of rulers and to make recommendations regarding policy. Just as those who paint landscapes set up their easels down in the valley in order to portray the nature of the mountains and the peaks, and climb up into the mountains in order to draw the valleys, similarly in order to properly understand the behavior of the lower classes one needs to be a ruler, and in order to properly understand the behavior of rulers one needs to be a member of the lower classes.

I therefore beg your Magnificence to accept this little gift in the spirit in which it is sent. If you read it carefully and think over what it contains, you will recognize it is an expression of my dearest wish, which is that you achieve the greatness your good fortune and your other fine qualities seem to hold out to you. And if your Magnificence, high up at the summit as you are, should occasionally glance down into these deep valleys, you will see I have to put up with the unrelenting malevolence of undeserved ill fortune.

Chapter One: How many types of principality are there? And how are they acquired?

All states, all forms of government that have had and continue to have authority over men, have been and are either republics or principalities. And principalities are either hereditary, when their rulers' ancestors have long been their rulers, or they are new. And if they are new, they are either entirely new, as was Milan for Francesco Sforza,[3] or they are like limbs added on to the hereditary state of the ruler who acquires them, as the kingdom of Naples has been added on to the kingdom of Spain.[4] Those dominions that are acquired by a ruler are either used to living under the rule of one man, or accustomed to being free; and they are either acquired with soldiers belonging to others, or with one's own; either through fortune or through strength [*virtù*].

Chapter Two: On hereditary principalities.

I will leave behind me the discussion of republics, for I have discussed them at length elsewhere. I will concern myself only with principalities.

3. Sforza acquired Milan in 1450. See below, chapter twelve.

4. Ferdinand the Catholic (1452–1516) acquired Naples in 1504. See below, chapters three and twenty-one.

The different types of principality I have mentioned will be the threads from which I will weave my account. I will debate how these different types of principality should be governed and defended.

I maintain, then, it is much easier to hold on to hereditary states, which are accustomed to being governed by the family that now rules them, than it is to hold on to new acquisitions. All one has to do is preserve the structures established by one's forebears, and play for time if things go badly. For, indeed, an hereditary ruler, if he is of no more than normal resourcefulness, will never lose his state unless some extraordinary and overwhelming force appears that can take it away from him; and even then, the occupier has only to have a minor setback, and the original ruler will get back to power.

Let us take a contemporary Italian example: The Duke of Ferrara was able to resist the assaults of the Venetians in '84, and of Pope Julius in 1510, only because his family was long established as rulers of that state. For a ruler who inherits power has few reasons and less cause to give offense; as a consequence he is more popular; and, as long as he does not have exceptional vices that make him hateful, it is to be expected he will naturally have the goodwill of his people. Because the state has belonged to his family from one generation to another, memories of how they came to power, and motives to overthrow them, have worn away. For every change in government creates grievances that those who wish to bring about further change can exploit.

Chapter Three: On mixed principalities.

New principalities are the ones that present problems. And first of all, if the whole of the principality is not new, but rather a new part has been added on to the old, creating a whole one may term "mixed," instability derives first of all from a natural difficulty that is to be found in all new principalities. The problem is that people willingly change their ruler, believing the change will be for the better; and this belief leads them to take up arms against him. But they are mistaken, and they soon find out in practice they have only made things worse. The reason for this, too, is natural and typical: You always have to give offense to those over whom you acquire power when you become a new ruler, both by imposing troops upon them, and by countless other injuries that follow as necessary consequences of the acquisition of power. Thus, you make enemies of all those to whom you have given offense in acquiring power, and in addition you cannot keep the good-will of those who have put you in power, for you cannot satisfy their aspirations as they thought you would. At the same time you cannot use heavy-handed methods against them, for you are obliged to them. Even if you have an overwhelmingly powerful army, you will have needed the support of the locals to take control of the province. This is why Louis XII of France lost Milan as quickly as he gained it.[5] All that was needed to take it from him the first time were Ludovico's own troops. For those who had opened the gates to him, finding themselves mistaken in their expectations and disappointed in their hopes of future benefit, could not put up with the burdensome rule of a new sovereign.

Of course it is true that, after a ruler has regained power in rebel territories, he is much more likely to hang on to it. For the rebellion gives him an excuse, and he is able to take firmer measures to secure his position, punishing delinquents, checking up on suspects, and taking precautions where needed. So, if the first time the King of France lost Milan all that was needed to throw him out was Duke Ludovico growling on his borders, to throw him out a second time it took the whole world united against him, and the destruction or expulsion from Italy of his armies.[6] We have seen why this was so.

Nevertheless, he lost Milan both times. We have discussed why he was almost bound to lose it the first time; now we must discuss why he managed to lose it the second. What remedies should he have adopted? What can someone in the King of France's position do to hold on to an acquisition more effectively than he did?

Let me start by saying these territories that are newly added on to a state that is already securely in the possession of a ruler are either in the same geographical region as his existing possessions and speak the same language, or they are not. When they are, it is quite straightforward to hold on to them, especially if they are not used to governing themselves. In order to get a secure hold on them one need merely eliminate the surviving members of the family of their previous rulers. In other respects one should keep things as they were, respecting established traditions. If the old territories and the new have similar customs, the new subjects will live quietly. Thus, Burgundy, Brittany, Gascony, and Normandy have for long quietly submitted to France. Although they do not all speak exactly the same language, nevertheless their customs are similar, and they can easily put up with each other.

5. Louis XII (1462–1515) became King of France in 1498 and invaded Italy in 1499. He gained Milan in February 1500 and lost it in April.

6. Louis regained Milan after the battle of Novara (April 1500), and lost it again after the Battle of Ravenna (April 1512). Ludovico Sforza (1451–1510), younger son of Francesco Sforza, ruled Milan from 1494 to 1500.

no change in lives

He who acquires neighboring territories in this way, intending to hold on to them, needs to see to two things: First, he must ensure their previous ruler has no heirs; and second, he must not alter their old laws or impose new taxes. If he follows these principles they will quickly become inseparable from his hereditary domains.

But when you acquire territories in a region that has a different language, different customs, and different institutions, then you really have problems, and you need to have great good fortune and great resourcefulness if you are going to hold on to them. One of the best policies, and one of the most effective, is for the new ruler to go and live in his new territories. This will make his grasp on them more secure and more lasting. This is what the Sultan of Turkey has done in Greece.[7] All the other measures he has taken to hold on to that territory would have been worthless if he had not settled there. For if you are on the spot, you can identify difficulties as they arise, and can quickly take appropriate action. If you are at a distance, you only learn of them when they have become serious, and when it is too late to put matters right. Moreover, if you are there in person, the territory will not be plundered by your officials. The subjects can appeal against their exactions to you, their ruler. As a consequence they have more reason to love you, if they behave themselves, and, if they do not, more reason to fear you. Anyone who wants to attack the territory from without will have to think twice, so that, if you live there, you will be unlucky indeed to lose it.

micro manage power

little corruption + clear + many

The second excellent policy is to send colonies to settle in one or two places; they will serve to tie your new subjects down. For it is necessary either to do this, or to garrison your new territory with a substantial army. Colonies do not cost much to run. You will have to lay out little or nothing to establish and maintain them. You will offend only those from whom you seize fields and houses to give to your settlers, and they will be only a tiny minority within the territory. Those whom you offend will be scattered and become poor, so they will be unable to do you any harm. All the rest will remain uninjured, and so ought to remain quiet; at the same time they will be afraid to make a false move, for they will have before them the fate of their neighbors as an example of what may happen to them. I conclude such colonies are economical, reliable, and do not give excessive grounds for resistance; those who suffer by their establishment are in no position to resist, being poor and scattered, as I have said. There is a general rule to be noted here: People should either be caressed or crushed. If you

7. Constantinople became capital of the Turkish empire in 1453.

[handwritten: small evils necessary]

do them minor damage they will get their revenge; but if you cripple them there is nothing they can do. If you need to injure someone, do it in such a way that you do not have to fear their vengeance.

But if, instead of establishing colonies, you rely on an occupying army, it costs a good deal more, for your army will eat up all your revenues from your new territory. As a result, your acquisition will be a loss, not a gain. Moreover, your army will make more enemies than colonies would, for the whole territory will suffer from it, the burden moving from one place to another as the troops are billeted first here, then there. Everybody suffers as a result, and everyone becomes your enemy. And these are enemies who can hurt you, for they remain, even if beaten, in their own homes. In every respect, then, an occupying army is a liability, while colonies are an asset. *[handwritten: belittle influence]*

In addition, anyone who finds himself with territory in a region with different customs from those of his hereditary possessions should make himself the leader and protector of neighboring powers who are weaker than he is, and should set out to weaken his powerful neighbors. He should also take care no outsider as powerful as himself has any occasion to intervene. Outside powers will always be urged to intervene by those in the region who are discontented, either because their ambitions are unsatisfied, or because they are afraid of the dominant powers. So, long ago, the Aetolians invited the Romans into Greece;[8] and, indeed, in every other region the Romans occupied they were invited by local people. It is in the nature of things that, as soon as a foreign power enters into a region, all the local states that are weak rally to it, for they are driven by the envy they have felt for the state that has exercised predominance over them. As a result, the invader does not have to make any effort at all to win over these lesser states, because they all immediately ally themselves to the territory he has acquired there. He only has to take care they do not become too strong and exercise too much influence. He can easily, with his own troops and his new allies' support, strike down the powerful states, and make himself the arbiter of all the affairs of the region. Anyone who does not see how to play this role successfully will quickly lose what he has gained, and, while he holds it, will have innumerable difficulties and vexations.

[handwritten: choose stronger for survival]

The Romans, in the regions they seized, obeyed these principles admirably. They settled colonies; were friendly towards the weaker rulers, without building up their strength; broke the powerful; and did not allow foreign powers to build up support. Let me take just the

8. 211 B.C. See Livy, bk. 26, ch. 24.

region of Greece as an example.[9] The Romans favored the Acheans and
the Aetolians; they crushed the Kingdom of Macedon; they expelled
Antiochus[10] from the region. Despite the credit the Acheans and the
Aetolians had earned with them, they never allowed them to build up
any independent power; nor did the blandishments of Philip[11] ever
persuade them to treat him as a friend before they had destroyed his
power; nor did Antiochus's strength intimidate them into permitting
him to retain any territory in that region.

/ this us paranoia?

The Romans did in such matters what all wise rulers ought to do.
It is necessary not only to pay attention to immediate crises, but to
foresee those that will come, and to make every effort to prevent them.
For if you see them coming well in advance, then you can easily take
the appropriate action to remedy them, but if you wait until they are
right on top of you, then the prescription will no longer take effect,
because the disease is too far advanced. In this matter it is as doctors
say of consumption: In the beginning the disease is easy to cure, difficult
to diagnose; but, after a while, if it has not been diagnosed and treated
early, it becomes easy to diagnose and hard to cure. So, too, in politics,
for if you foresee problems while they are far off (which only a prudent
man is able to do) they can easily be dealt with; but when, because
you have failed to see them coming, you allow them to grow to the
point that anyone can recognize them, then it is too late to do anything.

The Romans always looked ahead and took action to remedy problems before they developed. They never postponed action in order to
avoid a war, for they understood you cannot escape wars, and when
you put them off only your opponents benefit. Thus, they wanted to
have a war with Philip and Antiochus in Greece, so as not to have one
with them in Italy. At the time they could have avoided having a war
at all, but this they did not want. They never approved the saying that
nowadays is repeated *ad nauseam* by the wise: "Take advantage of
the passage of time." Rather they relied on their strength [*virtù*] and
prudence, for in time anything can happen, and the passage of time
brings good mixed with evil, and evil mixed with good.

But let us return to the kings of France, and let us see whether they
followed any of the principles I have outlined. I will discuss Louis, not
Charles, for, since Louis held territory in Italy for a longer time, we

9. The events to which Machiavelli refers occurred in 192 B.C. to 189 B.C.
See Livy, bk. 37.

10. Antiochus III, King of Syria.

11. Philip V of Macedon.

can have a better understanding of the policies he was following.[12] We will see he did the opposite of what one ought to do in order to hold on to territory in a region unlike one's hereditary lands.

King Louis was brought into Italy by the ambition of the Venetians, who hoped to gain half of the territory of Lombardy as a result of his invasion. I do not want to criticize the king's decision to ally with the Venetians. Since he wanted to get a foothold in Italy, and since he had no friends in that region (rather the opposite, for all the gateways to Italy were closed against him as a result of the actions of King Charles), he was obliged to take what allies he could get. His decision would have been a good one, if he had done everything else right. Now when the king had conquered Lombardy, he at once recovered the reputation Charles had lost for him. Genoa gave itself up and the Florentines became his friends. Everybody came forward to meet him as he advanced and sought his friendship: the Marquis of Mantua, the Duke of Ferrara, Bentivoglio, the Countess of Forlì, the rulers of Faenza, Pesaro, Rimini, Camerino, Piombino, the citizens of Lucca, Pisa, and Siena. Then the Venetians were able to see the risk they had chosen to run; in order to acquire a couple of fortresses in Lombardy, they had made the King of France master of two-thirds of Italy.

Now consider how easy it would have been for the king to preserve his authority in Italy if he had followed the principles I have laid out, and if he had protected and defended all his new friends. They were numerous, weak, and fearful, some afraid of the Church, some of the Venetians, and so had no choice but to remain loyal to him; and with their help he could easily have overwhelmed the surviving great powers. But he had no sooner got to Milan than he did the opposite, coming to the assistance of Pope Alexander so he could occupy the Romagna.[13] He did not realize that by this decision he weakened himself, alienating his friends and those who had flung themselves into his arms; and at the same time strengthened the Church, adding to its already extensive spiritual authority an increased temporal power. And having made one error he was forced to make another, for, in order to put a stop to Alexander's ambitions, and to prevent his gaining control of Tuscany, he was obliged to march into Italy once more. Nor was he satisfied with having strengthened the Church and thrown away his alliances,

12. Charles VIII (1470–98) ruled France from 1492 and invaded Italy in 1494. He was crowned King of Naples in 1494, but was forced out of Italy in 1495. Louis invaded Italy in 1499. His forces were decisively defeated at the Second Battle of Novara, 1512.

13. See below, chapter seven.

but in addition, because he wanted the Kingdom of Naples, he agreed
to divide it with the King of Spain.[14] Where he had been all-powerful
in Italy, he now shared his power with another, giving ambitious rulers
in the region and those who were discontented with him someone to
whom they could turn. Where he could have left in the Kingdom of
Naples a king who was on his payroll, he threw him out, and replaced
him with someone who might aspire to kick out the French.

It is perfectly natural and normal to want to acquire new territory;
and whenever men do what will succeed towards this end, they will
be praised, or at least not condemned. But when they are not in a
position to make gains, and try nevertheless, then they are making a
mistake, and deserve condemnation. If the King of France had the
military capacity to attack Naples, he should have done so; if he did
not have it, he should not have proposed to partition the territory. The
division of Lombardy between France and Venice was justified because
it gave the French a foothold in Italy; the division of Naples was
blameworthy, for it was not justifiable on the same grounds.

Thus, Louis had made the following five mistakes: He wasted his
alliance with the lesser states; he increased the strength of one of the
more powerful Italian states; he invited an extremely powerful foreign
state to intervene in Italy; he did not go and live in Italy; he did not
establish settlements there. Even these mistakes might have had no
evil consequences while he lived, had he not made a sixth, attacking
the Venetians. Had he not strengthened the Church and brought the
Spanish into Italy, then it would have been reasonable and appropriate
to attack them; but having done what he had done, he should never
have given his consent to a policy aimed at their destruction. For as
long as they remained powerful, the others would never have been
prepared to undertake an attack upon Lombardy. For the Venetians
would not have consented to Lombardy's falling into the hands of
others, and not themselves; while the others would not have wanted
to take Lombardy from the King of France only to give it to the
Venetians, and would not have had the courage to try to take it away
from both of them.

And if someone were to reply that King Louis allowed Alexander
to take the Romagna, and the King of Spain to have the Kingdom of
Naples, in order to avoid a war, I would answer as I did above: One
should never allow a problem to develop in order to avoid a war, for
you end up not avoiding the war, but deferring it to a time that will

14. Louis agreed to divide the Kingdom of Naples with Ferdinand the Catholic
in 1500, but lost the whole state to him in 1504.

be less favorable. And if others were to appeal to the promise the king had given to the pope, to help him seize the Romagna in return for the pope's giving him a divorce and making the Bishop of Rouen a cardinal, I would reply with what I will say later on the subject of whether and to what extent rulers should keep their word.

Thus, King Louis lost Lombardy because he did not follow any of the policies others have adopted when they have established predominance within a region and have wanted to hold on to it. There is nothing remarkable about what happened: It is entirely natural and predictable. I spoke about these matters with the Cardinal of Rouen in Nantes, when Valentino (as Cesare Borgia, son of Pope Alexander, was commonly called) was taking possession of the Romagna. The cardinal said to me that the Italians did not understand war; so I told him that the French did not understand politics, for if they did, they would not allow the church to acquire so much power. And in practice we have seen that the strength of the papacy and of the King of Spain within Italy has been brought about by the King of France, and they in turn have been the cause of his own ruin. From this one can draw a general conclusion that will never (or hardly ever) be proved wrong: He who is the cause of someone else's becoming powerful is the agent of his own destruction; for he makes his protegé powerful either through his own skill or through his own strength, and either of these must provoke his protegé's mistrust once he has become powerful.

Chapter Four: Why the kingdom of Darius, which Alexander occupied, did not rebel against his successors after Alexander's death.

When you think of the difficulties associated with trying to hold on to a newly acquired state, you might well be puzzled: Since Alexander the Great had conquered Asia in the space of a few years, and then died when he had scarcely had time to take possession of it, at that point you would expect the whole state to rebel.[15] Nevertheless, Alexander's successors maintained possession of it and had no difficulty in keeping hold of it, beyond the conflicts that sprung up between themselves as a result of their own ambitions. My explanation is that the principalities recorded in history have been governed in two different ways: either by a single individual, and everyone else has been his servant, and they have helped to govern his kingdom as ministers, appointed by his grace

15. Alexander conquered Asia between 334 and 327 B.C., and died in 323 B.C.

and benevolence; or by a monarch together with barons, who, not by concession of the ruler, but by virtue of their noble lineage, hold that rank. Such barons have their own territories and their own subjects: subjects who recognize them as their lords and feel a natural affection for them. In those states that are governed by a single individual and his servants, the sovereign has more authority in his own hands; for in all his territories there is no one recognized as having a right to rule except him alone; and if his subjects obey anyone else, they do so because he is the ruler's minister and representative, and they do not feel any particular loyalty to these subordinate authorities.

In our own day the obvious examples of these two types of ruler are the Sultan of Turkey and the King of France. All the kingdom of Turkey is ruled by a single monarch, and everyone else is his servant. He divides his kingdom into sanjaks,[16] sending administrators, whom he replaces and transfers as he thinks best, to rule them. But the King of France is placed among a multitude of long-established nobles, whose rights are recognized by their subjects and who are loved by them. They have their own inherited privileges, and the king cannot take them away without endangering himself. If you compare these two states, you will realize it would be difficult to seize the sultan's kingdom, but, once you had got control of it, it would be very easy to hold on to it.

It would be difficult to occupy the lands of the sultan for two reasons: The local authorities of that kingdom will not invite you to invade, nor can you hope those around the ruler will rebel, making your task easier. And this for the reasons I have explained. For, since they are all his slaves, and indebted to him, it is harder to corrupt them; and even if you can corrupt them, they are not going to be much use to you, for they cannot command the obedience of the people, as I have explained. Consequently, anyone attacking the sultan must expect to find the Turks united in his defense and must rely more on his own strength than on the disorder of his opponents. But once he has defeated them and has destroyed their forces on the field of battle so completely they cannot muster an army, then he has no one to worry about except the sultan's close relatives. Once he has got rid of them, then there is no one left for him to fear, for there is no one else with influence over the people. Just as the invader, before his victory, had no reason to hope for support, so, after his victory, he has no reason to fear opposition.

The opposite is true in kingdoms governed like that of France. For

16. An administrative region.

it is easy to invade them, once one has gained the support of some local noble. For in such kingdoms one can always find malcontents who hope to benefit from innovation. These, as we have seen, can ease your entrance into the state and help you win victory. But then, when you try to hold on to power, you will find the nobility, both those who have been your allies and those you have defeated, present you with an infinity of problems. It simply is not sufficient to kill the ruler and his close relatives, for the rest of the nobility will survive to provide leadership for new insurrections. You cannot win their loyalty or wipe them out, so you will always be in danger of losing your kingdom should anything go wrong.

Now if you ask yourself what sort of state it was Darius ruled, you will see it was similar to that of the sultan. So it was necessary for Alexander, first to take on his forces and seize control of the territory. Once he was victorious, and Darius was dead, Alexander had a firm grip on his new lands, for the reasons I have given. And his successors, if they had stayed united, could have enjoyed them at their leisure; nor was there any resistance to them in that kingdom, apart from their own conflicts with one another. But states that are organized after the French model cannot be held onto, once seized, with such ease. This is why there were frequent rebellions in Spain, France,[17] and Greece against the Romans. For there were many rulers in those territories, and as long as people remembered them, the Romans were always unsure of their grip. Once the memory of these rulers had faded completely away, thanks to the long duration of Roman rule, they became secure in their possession. Even after that, each faction among the Romans, when they fought among themselves, could call on the support of a section of those provinces, depending on the influence they had built up within them. The subjects of these territories, because their former rulers had no heirs, had no loyalties except to Roman leaders. Once you have considered all these matters, you will not be at all surprised at the ease with which Alexander held on to Asia or at the difficulties other conquerors (one might take Pyrrhus as one example among many) have had in keeping control of their acquisitions. The crucial factor in these differing outcomes is not the strength [*virtù*] or weakness of the conqueror but the contrasting character of the societies that have been conquered.

17. Machiavelli uses "France" to refer both to modern France and the ancient province of Gaul. Because one of his beliefs is that the French have not changed, I have kept his terminology as a reminder of his conviction that there is a real continuity between the ancient world and the present.

Chapter Five: How you should govern cities or kingdoms that,
before you acquired them, lived under their own laws.

When the states one acquires by conquest are accustomed to living
under their own laws and in freedom, there are three policies one can
follow in order to hold on to them: The first is to lay them waste; the
second is to go and live there in person; the third is to let them continue
to live under their own laws, make them pay you, and create there an
administrative and political elite who will remain loyal to you. For since
the elite are the creation of the head of state, its members know they
cannot survive without both his friendship and his power, and they
know it is in their interest to do everything to sustain it. It is easier to
rule a city that is used to being self-governing by employing its own
citizens than by other means, assuming you do not wish to destroy it.
   Examples are provided by the Spartans and the Romans. The Spartans took Athens and Thebes, establishing oligarchies there. However,
they lost them again.[18] The Romans, in order to hold on to Capua,
Carthage, and Numantia razed them and never lost them.[19] They
sought to govern Greece according to more or less the same policies
as those used by Sparta, letting the Greek cities rule themselves and
enforce their own laws, but the policy failed, so in the end they were
obliged to demolish many cities in that territory in order to hold on
to them. The simple truth is there is no reliable way of holding on to
a city and the territory around it, short of demolishing the city itself.
He who becomes the ruler of a city that is used to living under its own
laws and does not knock it down, must expect to be knocked down by
it. Whenever it rebels, it will find strength in the language of liberty
and will seek to restore its ancient constitution. Neither the passage
of time nor good treatment will make its citizens forget their previous
liberty. No matter what one does, and what precautions one takes, if
one does not scatter and drive away the original inhabitants, one will
not destroy the memory of liberty or the attraction of the old institutions.
As soon as there is a crisis, they will seek to restore them. This is what
happened in Pisa after it had been enslaved by the Florentines for a
hundred years.[20]
   But when cities or provinces are used to being ruled by a monarch,

18. The Spartan-sponsored oligarchies controlled Athens from 404 to 403
B.C. and Thebes from 382 to 379 B.C.

19. Capua in 211 B.C., Carthage in 146 B.C., Numantia in 133 B.C.

20. Pisa was controlled by Florence from 1406 to 1494, and recaptured in
1509.

ignorant

and one has wiped out his relatives and descendants, then matters are very different. They are used to being obedient. Their old ruler is gone, and they cannot agree among themselves as to who should replace him. They do not know how to rule themselves. The result is that they are slower to take up arms, and it is easier for a new ruler to win them over and establish himself securely in power. But in former republics there is more vitality, more hatred, more desire for revenge. The memory of their former freedom gives them no rest, no peace. So the best thing to do is to demolish them or to go and live there oneself.

Chapter Six: About new kingdoms acquired with one's own armies and one's own skill [*virtù*].

No one should be surprised if, in talking about completely new kingdoms (that is, states that are governed by someone who was not a ruler before, and were themselves not previously principalities), I point to the greatest of men as examples to follow. For men almost always walk along the beaten path, and what they do is almost always an imitation of what others have done before. But you cannot walk exactly in the footsteps of those who have gone before, nor is it easy to match the skill [*virtù*] of those you have chosen to imitate. Consequently, a prudent man will always try to follow in the footsteps of great men and imitate those who have been truly outstanding, so that, if he is not quite as skillful [*virtù*] as they, at least some of their ability may rub off on him. One should be like an experienced archer, who, trying to hit someone at a distance and knowing the range [*virtù*] of his bow, aims at a point above his target, not so his arrow will strike the point he is aiming at, but so, by aiming high, he can reach his objective.

I maintain that, in completely new kingdoms, the new ruler has more or less difficulty in keeping hold of power depending on whether he is more or less skillful [*virtuoso*]. Now you only find yourself in this situation, a private individual only becomes a ruler, if you are either lucky, or skillful [*virtù*]. Both luck and skill enable you to overcome difficulties. Nevertheless, he who relies least on luck has the best prospect of success. One advantage is common to any completely new sovereign: Because he has no other territories, he has no choice but to come in person and live in his new kingdom. Let us look at those who through their own skill [*virtù*], and not merely through chance, have become rulers. In my view, the greatest have been Moses, Cyrus, Romulus, Theseus, and others like them.[21]

21. Cyrus overcame the Medes around 550 B.C. and founded the Persian Empire. Romulus is the mythical founder of Rome, and Theseus the slayer

Obviously, we should not discuss Moses' skill, for he was a mere agent, following the instructions given him by God. So he should be admired, not for his own skill, but for that grace that made him worthy to talk with God. But let us discuss Cyrus and the others who have acquired existing kingdoms or founded new ones. You will find them all admirable. And if you look at the actions and strategies of each one of them, you will find they do not significantly differ from those of Moses, who could not have had a better teacher. If you look at their deeds and their lives, you will find they were dependent on chance only for their first opportunity. They seized their chance to make of it what they wanted. Without that first opportunity their strength [*virtù*] of purpose would never have been revealed. Without their strength [*virtù*] of purpose, the opportunity they were offered would not have amounted to anything.

Thus, it was necessary for Moses to find the people of Israel in Egypt, enslaved and oppressed by the Egyptians, so they, in order to escape from slavery, would be prepared to follow him. It was essential for Romulus to have no future in Alba, it was appropriate he should have been exposed at birth, otherwise he would not have formed the ambition of becoming King of Rome and succeeded in founding that nation. It was necessary that Cyrus should find the Persians hostile to the rule of the Medes, and the Medes weak and effeminate from too much peace. Theseus could not have demonstrated his strength of purpose [*virtù*] if he had not found the Athenians scattered. These opportunities made these men lucky; but it was their remarkable political skill [*virtù*] that enabled them to recognize these opportunities for what they were. Thanks to them their nations were ennobled and blessed with good fortune.

Those who become rulers through strength of purpose [*vie virtuose*], as they did, acquire their kingdoms with difficulty, but they hold on to them with ease. And much of the difficulty they have in getting to power derives from the new institutions and customs they are obliged to establish in order to found their governments and make them secure. One ought to pause and consider the fact that there is nothing harder to undertake, nothing more likely of failure, nothing more risky to pull off, than to set oneself up as a leader who plans to found a new system of government. For the founder makes enemies of all those who are doing well under the old system, and has only lukewarm support from those who hope to do well under the new one. The weakness of their

---

of the Minotaur and founder of Athens (1234 B.C.): Machiavelli took them to be genuine historical persons.

support springs partly from their fear of their adversaries, who have the law on their side, partly from their own want of faith. For men do not truly believe in new things until they have had practical experience of them. So it is that, whenever those who are enemies of the new order have a chance to attack it, they do so ferociously, while the others defend it half-heartedly. So the new ruler is in danger, along with his supporters.

It is necessary, however, if we are going to make sense of his situation, to find out if our innovator stands on his own feet, or depends on others to prop him up. That is, we need to know if he is obliged to try to obtain his objectives by pleading, or whether he can resort to force. In the first case, he is bound to come to a bad end, and won't achieve anything. But when he can stand on his own feet, and can resort to force, the ` he can usually overcome the dangers he faces. Thus it is that all armed prophets are victorious, and disarmed ones are crushed. For there is another problem: People are by nature inconstant. It is easy to persuade them of something, but it is difficult to stop them from changing their minds. So you have to be prepared for the moment when they no longer believe: Then you have to force them to believe. Moses, Cyrus, Theseus, and Romulus would not have been able to make their peoples obey their new structures of authority for long if they had been unarmed. This is what happened, in our own day, to Friar Girolamo Savonarola.[22] He and his new constitution were destroyed as soon as the multitude began to stop believing in him. He had no way of stiffening the resolution of those who had been believers or of forcing disbelievers to obey.

Thus the founders of new states have immense difficulties to overcome, and dangers beset their path, dangers they must overcome by skill and strength of purpose [*virtù*]. But, once they have overcome them, and they have begun to be idolized, having got rid of those who were jealous of their superior qualities, they are established, they are powerful, secure, honored, happy.

We have looked at some noble examples, and to them I want to add one less remarkable. Nevertheless, it has some points of similarity to them, and I want it to stand for all the other lesser examples I could have chosen. My example is Hiero of Syracuse.[23] He was a private

22. Girolamo Savonarola (b. 1452) was a Dominican friar and prophetic preacher. He dominated Florentine politics from the expulsion of the Medici in 1494 until 1498, when he was executed as a heretic.

23. Hiero II became King of Syracuse in 269 B.C. Machiavelli's sources are Polybius, bk. 7, ch. 8, and Justin, bk. 23, ch. 4.

individual who became ruler of Syracuse. He, too, did not depend on luck once he had been given his opportunity. The people of Syracuse were oppressed and elected him as their military commander; so he deserved to be made their ruler. He was so remarkable [*di tanta virtù*], even before he became a ruler, history records "that he had everything one would look for in a king, except a kingdom." He disbanded the old militia and instituted a new one. Dropped his old friends and chose new ones. Since both his friends and his soldiers were his creatures, he had laid the foundations for constructing any political system he chose. He, too, had difficulties enough to overcome in acquiring power, and few in holding on to it.

Chapter Seven: About new principalities that are acquired with the forces of others and with good luck.

Those who, having started as private individuals, become rulers merely out of good luck, acquire power with little trouble but have a hard time holding on to it. They have no problems on the road to power, because they leap over all the obstacles; but dangers crowd around them once they are in power. I am talking about people who are given a state, either in return for money, or out of the goodwill of him who hands it over to them. This happened to many individuals in Greece, in the cities of Ionia and the Hellespont, who were made rulers by Darius, who wanted them to hold their cities for his own greater safety and glory.[24] So, too, with those who, having been private citizens, were made emperors of Rome because they had corrupted the soldiers.[25] Such rulers are entirely dependent on the goodwill and good fortune of whoever has given them power. Good will and good fortune are totally unreliable and capricious. Such rulers do not know how to hold on to their position and cannot do so. They do not know how, because they have always been private citizens, and only a brilliant and immensely skillful [*di grande virtù*] man is likely to know how to command without having had training and experience. They cannot because they have no troops of their own on whose loyalty and commitment they can count.

Moreover, states that spring up overnight, like all other things in nature that are born and grow in a hurry, cannot have their roots deep in the soil, so they shrivel up in the first drought, blow over in the first

24. Machiavelli is refering to Greek-speaking cities in Asia and the Hellespont in the sixth century B.C.

25. See below, chapter nineteen.

storm. Unless, as I have said, those who are suddenly made into rulers are of such extraordinary capacity [*virtù*] they can work out on the spot how to hold on to the gift fortune has unexpectedly handed them; and those preparations the others made before they became rulers, they must find a way of making after the event.

I want to add to the one and the other of these two ways of becoming a ruler, by skill [*virtù*] or by luck, two examples drawn from the events that have occurred in our own lifetimes: the examples of Francesco Sforza and Cesare Borgia. Francesco, by using the right methods and consummate skill [*virtù*], started out as a private citizen and ended up as Duke of Milan. And what he had acquired with painstaking effort, he held on to without trouble.[26] On the other hand Cesare Borgia, who was called Duke Valentino by the common people, acquired his state thanks to the good fortune of his father, and when that came to an end he lost it.[27] This despite the fact he used every technique and did all the things a prudent and skillful [*virtuoso*] man ought to do, to entrench himself in those territories that the arms and fortune of others had acquired for him. For, as I said above, he who does not prepare the foundations first can (in principle), if he is immensely skillful [*virtù*], make up for it later, although the architect will find catching up a painful process, and there is a real danger the building will collapse. So, if we look at all the things Borgia did, we will see he had laid solid foundations for future power. I do not think it irrelevant to discuss his policies, because I cannot think of any better example I could offer a new ruler than that of his actions. And if his strategy did not lead to success, this was not his fault; his failure was due to extraordinary and exceptional hostility on the part of fortune.

Pope Alexander VI, in setting out to make his son the duke into a ruler, was faced with considerable immediate and long-term difficulties. In the first place, he could find no way of making him the lord of any territory, except territory that belonged to the church. And he knew if he took land from the church to give to Cesare, he would have to overcome the opposition of the Duke of Milan, and also of the Venetians, for both Faenza and Rimini were already under Venetian protection. Secondly, he saw the armed forces of Italy, and particularly those he could hope to employ, were under the control of individuals who had reason to fear any increase in papal power. Consequently, he could

26. See below, chapter twelve.
27. Cesare Borgia (1475–1507) was the natural son of Rodrigo Borgia (1431–1503), who became Pope Alexander VI in 1492. He began the conquest of the Romagna in 1499.

not regard them as reliable. He could not trust the Orsini, the Colonna, or their associates, but there was no one else to whom he could turn.[28] So it was necessary to break out of this framework, and to bring disorder to the territories of his opponents, so he could safely seize a part of them. This proved easy, for he found the Venetians, for reasons of their own, had decided to invite the French to invade Italy. He not only did not oppose this, but he facilitated it by dissolving the previous marriage of King Louis. So the king marched into Italy, with the help of the Venetians and the consent of Alexander. No sooner was he in Milan than the pope had borrowed forces from him for the attack on the Romagna, which was ceded to him out of fear of the King of France.

So, once Cesare had been made Duke of the Romagna, and the Colonnesi had been beaten, wanting to hang on to his new territories and make further conquests, he was faced with two obstacles. In the first place, his military forces did not appear reliable. In the second, the King of France might oppose him. He had made use of the troops of the Orsini, but they were likely to abandon him, and not only prevent him from making further acquisitions, but take from him what he had already acquired. And the same was true of the king. He had an indication of how far he could trust the Orsini when, after Faenza had been taken by storm, he attacked Bologna, for he discovered they had no appetite for that battle.[29] And as for the king, he discovered his attitude when, having seized the Duchy of Urbino, he attacked Tuscany, for Louis made him abandon that enterprise.[30] So the duke decided he must no longer depend on the troops and the good fortune of others.

The first thing he did was to weaken the factions of the Orsini and the Colonna in Rome. All the nobles who were allied to these families he won over to himself, making them members of his court, and giving them substantial pensions. He favored them with civil and military appointments appropriate to their standing. Thus, in the course of a few months, their attachment to their factions was dissolved, and they became committed to the duke. Next, he looked for a chance to crush the Orsini, having already defeated the forces of the Colonna family. He soon had his chance and he made the most of it. For the Orsini, having realized late in the day that the growing strength of the duke and the pope would be their ruin, called a meeting at Magione, near

28. On the Orsini and the Colonna, see below, chapter eleven.

29. In the spring of 1501.

30. In the summer of 1502.

Perugia. From that meeting sprang the rebellion of Urbino and the uprisings in the Romagna that almost destroyed the duke; but he overcame all resistance with the help of the French.[31] And, having got back his authority and realizing he could trust neither the French nor other external forces, he decided that, in order to prevent their allying against him, he must deceive them. He so successfully concealed his intentions that the Orsini, represented by Signor Paolo, made peace with him. The duke took every opportunity to ingratiate himself with Paolo, giving him money, clothes, and horses. So the leaders of the Orsini were brought, unsuspecting, to Sinigallia, where they were at his mercy.[32] Having got rid of the leaders and won the allegiance of their followers, the duke could feel he had laid decent foundations for his future power. He had control of all the Romagna and the Duchy of Urbino, and it looked as though he had won over the Romagna and acquired the support of its population, who were beginning to enjoy a new prosperity.

Now, since it is worth paying attention to this question, and since it would be sensible to imitate Cesare's actions, I want to amplify what I have just said. Once the duke had subdued the Romagna, he found it had been under the control of weak nobles, who had rather exploited than governed their subjects and had rather been the source of conflict than of order, with the result the whole province was full of robbers, bandits, and every other type of criminal. So he decided it was necessary, if he was going to make the province peaceful and obedient to his commands, to give it good government. He put Mr. Remiro d'Orco, a man both cruel and efficient, in charge, and gave him absolute power. D'Orco in short order established peace and unity, and acquired immense authority. At that point, the duke decided such unchecked power was no longer necessary, for he feared people might come to hate it. So he established a civil court in the center of the province, placing an excellent judge in charge of it, and requiring every city to appoint a lawyer to represent it before the court. Since he knew the harsh measures of the past had given rise to some enmity towards him, in order to purge the ill-will of the people and win them completely over to him, he wanted to make clear that, if there had been any cruelty, he was not responsible for it, and that his hard-hearted minister should be blamed. He saw his opportunity and exploited it. One morning, in the town square of Cesena, he had Remiro d'Orco's corpse laid out

31. October 1502.

32. They were captured on 31 December 1502. Some were killed at once; others a few weeks later.

in two pieces, with a chopping board and a bloody knife beside it.[33] This ferocious sight made the people of the Romagna simultaneously happy and dumbfounded.

But let us get back to where we were. I was saying the duke found himself rather powerful and had taken precautions against immediate dangers, for he had built up a military force that he had planned himself and had in large part destroyed neighboring forces that could be a threat to him. So what remained, if he wanted to make further acquisitions, was the problem of the King of France; for he knew the king had, late in the day, realized his policy towards Borgia had been misconceived and would not allow him to make further conquests. So Borgia began to look for new alliances and to prevaricate with the French when they dispatched a force towards the Kingdom of Naples to attack the Spanish who were laying siege to Gaeta.[34] His intention was to protect himself against them, which he would soon have succeeded in doing, if Alexander had gone on living.

These were the policies he pursued with regard to his immediate concerns. But there were future problems he also had to consider. In the first place, he had to worry that a new pope would be hostile to him and would try to take from him what Alexander had given him. He had four ways of trying to deal with this threat. In the first place, he set out to eliminate all the relatives of those rulers whose lands he had seized, to make it difficult for the pope to restore their previous rulers. Second, he sought to acquire the allegiance of the nobility of Rome, as I have explained, so he could use them to restrict the pope's freedom of action. Third, to make as many as possible of the members of the College of Cardinals his allies. Fourth, to acquire so much power, before the pope died, that he would be able on his own to resist a first attack. Of these four policies he had successfully carried out three by the time Alexander died; the fourth he had almost accomplished. Of the rulers he had dispossessed, he murdered as many as he could get his hands on, and only a very few survived. The Roman nobility were his supporters, and he had built up a very large faction in the College of Cardinals. As far as new acquisitions were concerned, he had plans for conquering Tuscany; he already held Perugia and Piombino; and he had taken Pisa under his protection. And, as soon as he would no longer have to worry about the King of France (which was already the case, for the French had already lost the Kingdom of Naples to the Spanish, with the result that both France and Spain were now obliged

33. 26 December 1502.
34. 1503.

to try to buy his friendship), he would be free to seize Pisa. After which, Lucca and Siena would quickly give in, partly because they hated the Florentines, and partly because they would have been terrified. The Florentines could have done nothing.

If he had succeeded in all this (and he was on the point of succeeding in the very year Alexander died) he would have acquired so much strength and so much authority he would have become his own master. He would no longer have depended on events outside his control and on the policies of others, but would have been able to rely on his own power and strength [*virtù*]. But Alexander died only five years after Cesare Borgia had unsheathed his sword.[35] He found himself with only his control over the Romagna firmly established, with everything else up in the air, caught between two powerful hostile armies, and dangerously ill. But the duke was so pugnacious and so strong [*virtù*], he so well understood what determines whether one wins or loses, and he had laid such sound foundations within such a short time, that, if he had not had these enemy armies breathing down his neck, or if he had been in good health, he could have overcome every difficulty.

I am justified in claiming he had laid sound foundations, for the Romagna remained loyal to him in his absence for more than a month; in Rome, although he was half dead, he was quite safe, and although the Ballioni, the Vitelli, and the Orsini congregated in Rome, they could not muster a following to attack him; and, if he was not in a position to choose who should be pope, he could at least veto anyone he did not trust. So, if he had been well when Alexander died he would have been able to deal with his problems without difficulty. He told me himself, on the day Julius II was elected,[36] that he had asked himself what he would do if his father died and had been confident he could handle the situation, but that it had never occurred to him that when his father died he himself would be at death's door.

So, now I have surveyed all the actions of the duke, I still cannot find anything to criticize. It seems to me I have been right to present him as an example to be imitated by all those who come to power through good luck and thanks to someone else's military might. For, since he was great-hearted and ambitious, he had no choice as to what to do; and he only failed to achieve his goals because Alexander died

35. 18 August 1503.

36. 28 October 1503. Giuliano della Rovere (1443–1513) had been appointed Cardinal of San Piero ad Vincula in 1471, when his uncle became Pope Sixtus IV. For Machiavelli's assessment of his papacy, see below, chapters eleven and twenty-five.

too soon, and he himself fell ill. So anyone who decides that the policy to follow when one has newly acquired power is to destroy one's enemies, to secure some allies, to win wars, whether by force or by fraud, to make oneself both loved and feared by one's subjects, to make one's soldiers loyal and respectful, to wipe out those who can or would want to hurt one, to innovate, replacing old institutions with new practices, to be both harsh and generous, magnanimous and open-handed, to disband disloyal troops and form new armies, to build alliances with other powers, so kings and princes either have to win your favor or else think twice before going against your wishes—anyone who thinks in these terms cannot hope to find, in the recent past, a better model to imitate than Cesare Borgia.

His only mistake was to allow Julius to be elected pope, for there he made a bad choice. The choice was his to make, for as I have said, if he could not choose who should be pope, he could veto anyone he did not like, and he should never have agreed to any cardinal's being elected with whom he had been in conflict in the past, or who, once he had been elected, would have been likely to be afraid of him. For men attack either out of fear or out of hatred. Those who had scores to settle with him included San Piero ad Vincula, Colonna, San Giorgio, Ascanio; all the others, if elected pope, would have had good reason to fear him, with the exception of Rouen and of the Spanish cardinals. The Spanish were his relatives and allies; Rouen was powerful, having the support of the King of France. So the duke's first objective should have been to ensure a Spaniard was elected pope; failing that, he should have agreed to the election of Rouen and vetoed that of San Piero ad Vincula. If he imagined recent gestures of goodwill make the powerful forget old injuries, he was much mistaken. So the duke made a mistake during the election of the pope, and this mistake was, in the end, the cause of his destruction.

Chapter Eight: Of those who come to power through wicked
                 actions.

But since there are two other ways a private citizen can become a ruler, two ways that do not simply involve the acquisition of power either through fortune or strength [*virtù*], I feel I cannot omit discussion of them, although one of them can be more fully treated elsewhere, where I discuss republics. These are, first, when one acquires power through some wicked or nefarious action, and second when a private citizen becomes ruler of his own country because he has the support of his fellow citizens. Here I will talk about the first of these two routes to power, and will use two examples, one ancient, one modern, to show how it is done. These will be sufficient, I trust, to provide a model for anyone who has no alternative options. I do not intend to discuss in detail the rights and wrongs of such a policy.

Agathocles of Sicily became King of Syracuse, although he was not merely a private citizen, but of humble and poverty-stricken origins.[37] He was the son of a potter, and from start to finish lived a wicked life; nevertheless, his wicked behavior testified to so much strength [*virtù*] of mind and of body that, when he joined the army, he was promoted through the ranks to the supreme command. Having risen so high, he decided to become the sole ruler and to hold on to power, which he had originally been granted by the consent of his fellow citizens, by violence and without being dependent on anyone else. Having entered into a conspiracy with a Carthaginian called Hamilcar, who was commander of a hostile army serving in Sicily, one morning he called together the people and the senate of Syracuse, as if he wanted to discuss matters of government policy, and, at a prearranged signal, had his soldiers kill all the senators and the richest citizens. With them out of the way, he made himself ruler of the city and held power without any resistance. Although the Carthaginians twice defeated his armies and even advanced to the walls of the city, he was not only able to defend his city, but, leaving part of his army behind to withstand the siege, he was able to attack the Carthaginians in Africa with the remainder of his forces. Within a short time he had forced them to lift the siege and was threatening to conquer Carthage. In the end they were obliged to come to terms with him, leaving Sicily to Agathocles in return for security in Africa.

If you consider Agathocles' bold achievements [*azioni e virtù*], you will not find much that can be attributed to luck; for, as I have said, he did not come to power because he had help from above, but because he worked his way up from below, climbing from rank to rank by undergoing infinite dangers and discomforts until in the end he obtained a monopoly of power, and then holding on to his position by bold and risky tactics.

One ought not, of course, to call it *virtù* [virtue or manliness] to massacre one's fellow citizens, to betray one's friends, to break one's word, to be without mercy and without religion. By such means one can acquire power but not glory. If one considers the manly qualities [*virtù*] Agathocles demonstrated in braving and facing down danger,

37. Agathocles (361–289 B.C.) seized control of Syracuse in 317 B.C. Machiavelli's source is Justin, bk. 22.

and the strength of character he showed in surviving and overcoming adversity, then there seems to be no reason why he should be judged less admirable than any of the finest generals. But on the other hand, his inhuman cruelty and brutality, and his innumerable wicked actions, mean it would be wrong to praise him as one of the finest of men. It is clear, at any rate, that one can attribute neither to luck nor to virtue [*virtù*] his accomplishments, which owed nothing to either.

In our own day, when Alexander VI was pope, Oliverotto of Fermo, whose father had died a few years before, was raised by his maternal uncle, Giovanni Fogliani.[38] As soon as he was old enough he joined the forces of Paolo Vitelli, so that, with a good military training, he could pursue a career in the army.[39] When Paolo died, he signed up with his brother, Vitellozzo. In a very short time, because he was bright and had both a strong body and a lively spirit, he became Vitellozzo's second-in-command. Soon he thought it to be beneath his dignity to serve under another, and so he conspired to occupy Fermo, relying on the help of some citizens of that city who preferred to see their fatherland enslaved than free, and on the support of Vitellozzo. He wrote to his uncle, saying that, since he had been away from home for many years, he wanted to come to visit him and to see his city, and so, in a manner of speaking, reacquaint himself with his inheritance. He said he had only gone to war in order to acquire honor. So his fellow citizens would be able to see he had not been wasting his time, he wanted to arrive in state, accompanied by a hundred men on horseback, some of them his friends, and others his servants. He asked his uncle to ensure that the inhabitants of Fermo received him with respect: This would enhance not only his reputation, but that of his uncle, who raised him.

Giovanni did everything he could for his nephew. He ensured he was greeted by the people of Fermo with every honor, and he put him up in his own house. After a few days had gone by, and he had had time to make the arrangements necessary for the carrying out of his wicked plans, he held a lavish banquet at his uncle's, to which he invited his uncle and the most powerful citizens of Fermo. After the food had been eaten, and the guests had been entertained in all the ways that are customary upon such occasions, Oliverotto deliberately began discussing serious questions, talking about the greatness of Pope

38. Oliverotto Euffreducci (b. ca. 1475) seized Fermo in 1501. Borgia had him killed at Sinigallia in December 1502.

39. The Florentines made Vitelli commander of their forces in 1498 and executed him in 1499. See below, chapter twelve.

Alexander and his son Cesare, and about their undertakings. When his uncle Giovanni and the others picked up the subject, he sprang to his feet, saying such matters should be discussed in a more private place. He withdrew into another room, where Giovanni and all the other leading citizens followed. No sooner had they sat down than soldiers emerged from their hiding places and killed Giovanni along with all the rest. Once the killing was over, Oliverotto got on his horse and took possession of the city, laying siege to the government building. Those in authority were so terrified they agreed to obey him and to establish a new regime of which he was the head. With all those who had something to lose and would have been able to resist him dead, he was able to entrench himself by establishing new civilian and military institutions. Within a year of coming to power, he was not only securely in control of Fermo, but had become a threat to all the cities round about. It would soon have been as difficult to get rid of him as to get rid of Agathocles, had he not allowed himself to be taken in by Cesare Borgia, when, as I have already explained, he got rid of the Orsini and the Vitelli at Sinigallia. Oliverotto was seized at the same time, and, a year after he had killed his uncle, he was strangled along with Vitellozzo from whom he had learned how to be bold [*virtù*] and how to be wicked.

Perhaps you are wondering how Agathocles and others like him, despite their habitual faithlessness and cruelty, have been able to live safely in their homelands year after year, and to defend themselves against their enemies abroad. Why did their fellow subjects not conspire against them? After all, mere cruelty has not been enough to enable many other rulers to hang on to power even in time of peace, let alone during the turmoil of war. I think here we have to distinguish between cruelty well used and cruelty abused. Well-used cruelty (if one can speak well of evil) one may call those atrocities that are committed at a stroke, in order to secure one's power, and are then not repeated, rather every effort is made to ensure one's subjects benefit in the long run. An abuse of cruelty one may call those policies that, even if in the beginning they involve little bloodshed, lead to more rather than less as time goes by. Those who use cruelty well may indeed find both God and their subjects are prepared to let bygones be bygones, as was the case with Agathocles. Those who abuse it cannot hope to retain power indefinitely.

So the conclusion is: If you take control of a state, you should make a list of all the crimes you have to commit and do them all at once. That way you will not have to commit new atrocities every day, and you will be able, by not repeating your evil deeds, to reassure your subjects and to win their support by treating them well. He who acts otherwise, either out of squeamishness or out of bad judgment, has to hold a bloody knife in his hand all the time. He can never rely on his subjects, for they can never trust him, for he is always making new attacks upon them. Do all the harm you must at one and the same time, that way the full extent of it will not be noticed, and it will give least offense. One should do good, on the other hand, little by little, so people can fully appreciate it.

A ruler should, above all, behave towards his subjects in such a way that, whatever happens, whether for good or ill, he has no need to change his policies. For if you fall on evil times and are obliged to change course, you will not have time to benefit from the harm you do, and the good you do will do you no good, because people will think you have been forced to do it, and they will not be in the slightest bit grateful to you.

Chapter Nine: Of the citizen-ruler.

But, coming to the alternative possibility, when a private citizen becomes the ruler of his homeland, not through wickedness or some act of atrocity, but through the support of his fellow citizens, so that we may call him a citizen-ruler (remember we are discussing power acquired neither by pure strength [*virtù*] nor mere luck—in this case one needs a lucky cunning), I would point out there are two ways to such power: the support of the populace or the favor of the elite. For in every city one finds these two opposed classes. They are at odds because the populace do not want to be ordered about or oppressed by the elite; and the elite want to order about and oppress the populace. The conflict between these two irreconcilable ambitions has in each city one of three possible consequences: rule by one man, liberty, or anarchy.

Rule by one man can be brought about either by the populace or the elite, depending on whether one or the other of these factions hopes to benefit from it. For if the elite fear they will be unable to control the populace, they begin to build up the reputation of one of their own, and they make him sole ruler in order to be able, under his protection, to achieve their objectives. The populace on the other hand, if they fear they are going to be crushed by the elite, build up the reputation of one of their number and make him sole ruler, in order that his authority may be employed in their defense. He who comes to power with the help of the elite has more difficulty in holding on to power than he who comes to power with the help of the populace, for in the former case he is surrounded by many who think of themselves as his equals, and whom he consequently cannot order about or manipulate as he might wish. He who comes to power with the support of the populace, on the other hand, has it all to himself: There is no one, or hardly anyone, around him who is not prepared to obey. In addition, one cannot honorably give the elite what they want, and one cannot do it without harming others; but this is not true with the populace, for the objectives of the populace are less immoral than those of the elite, for the latter want to oppress, and the former not to be oppressed. Thirdly, if the masses are opposed to you, you can never be secure, for there are too many of them; but the elite, since there are few of them, can be neutralized.

The worst a ruler who is opposed by the populace has to fear is that they will give him no support; but from the elite he has to fear not only lack of support, but worse, that they will attack him. For the elite have more foresight and more cunning; they act in time to protect themselves, and seek to ingratiate themselves with rivals for power. Finally, the ruler cannot get rid of the populace but must live with them; he can, however, get by perfectly well without the members of the elite, being able to make and unmake them each day, and being in a position to give them status or take it away, as he chooses.

In order to clarify the issues, let me point out there are two principal points of view from which one should consider the elite. Either they behave in a way that ties their fortunes to yours, or they do not. Those who tie themselves to you and are not rapacious, you should honor and love; those who do not tie themselves to you are to be divided into two categories. If they retain their independence through pusillanimity and because they are lacking in courage, then you should employ them, especially if they have good judgment, for you can be sure they will help you achieve success so long as things are going well for you, and you can also be confident you have nothing to fear from them if things go badly. But if they retain their independence from you out of calculation and ambition, then you can tell they are more interested in their own welfare than yours. A ruler must protect himself against such people and fear them as much as if they were publicly declared enemies, for you can be sure that, in adversity, they will help to overthrow you.

Anyone who becomes a ruler with the support of the populace ought to ensure he keeps their support; which will not be difficult, for all they ask is not to be oppressed. But anyone who becomes a ruler with the support of the elite and against the wishes of the populace must above all else seek to win the populace over to his side, which will be easy to do if he protects their interests. And since people, when they are well-treated by someone whom they expected to treat them badly, feel all the more obliged to their benefactor, he will find that the populace will quickly become better inclined towards him than if he had come to power with their support. There are numerous ways the ruler can win the support of the populace. They vary so much depending on the circumstances they cannot be reduced to a formula, and, consequently, I will not go into them here. I will simply conclude by saying a ruler needs to have the support of the populace, for otherwise he has nothing to fall back on in times of adversity.

Nabis, ruler of the Spartans, survived an attack by the confederate forces of all Greece, together with an almost invincible Roman army, and successfully defended both his homeland and his own hold on power. All he needed to do, when faced with danger, was neutralize a few; but if he had had the populace opposed to him, this would have been insufficient.[40] Do not think you can rebut my argument by citing the well-worn proverb, "Relying on the people is like building on the sand." This is quite true when a private citizen depends upon them and gives the impression he expects the populace to free him if he is seized by his enemies or by the magistrates. In such a case one can easily find oneself disappointed, as happened to the Gracchi in Rome and to Mr. Giorgio Scali in Florence.[41] But if you are a ruler and you put your trust in the populace, if you can give commands and are capable of bold action, if you are not nonplused by adversity, if you take other necessary precautions, and if through your own courage and your policies you keep up the morale of the populace, then you will never be let down by them, and you will discover you have built on a sound foundation.

The type of one-man rule we are discussing tends to be at risk at the moment of transition from constitutional to dictatorial government. Such rulers either give commands in their own name, or act through the officers of state. In the second case, their situation is more dangerous and less secure. For they are entirely dependent on the cooperation of those citizens who have been appointed to the offices of state, who can, particularly at times of crisis, easily deprive them of their power, either by directly opposing them or by simply failing to carry out their instructions. It is too late for the ruler once a crisis is upon him to seize dictatorial authority, for the citizens and the subjects, who are

40. Nabis (ca. 240–192 B.C.) became ruler of Sparta in 207 B.C. Livy (bk. 34) puts the number assassinated at eighty.

41. The Gracchi brothers (Tiberius Sempronius [163–133 B.C.] and Gaius Sempronius [153–121 B.C.]) were advocates of agrarian reform who both died in riots. Scali was a populist leader in Florence during the Ciompi rising of 1378 but was executed for an attack on the authorities in 1382.

used to obeying the constituted authorities, will not, in such circumstances, obey him, and he will always have, in difficult circumstances, a shortage of people on whom he can rely. For such a ruler cannot expect things to continue as they were when there were no difficulties, when all the citizens are conscious of what the government can do for them. Then everyone flocked round, everyone promised support, everyone was willing to die for him, when there was no prospect of having to do so. But when times are tough, when the government is dependent on its citizens, then there will be few who are prepared to stand by it. One does not learn the danger of such an erosion of support from experience, as the first experience proves fatal. So a wise ruler will seek to ensure that his citizens always, no matter what the circumstances, have an interest in preserving both him and his authority. If he can do this, they will always be faithful to him.

Chapter Ten: How one should measure the strength of a ruler.

There is another factor one should take into account when categorizing rulers: One should ask if a ruler has enough resources to be able, if necessary, to look after himself, or whether he will always be dependent on having alliances with other rulers. In order to clarify this question, I would maintain those rulers can look after themselves who have sufficient reserves, whether of troops or of money, to be able to put together a sound army and face battle against any opponent. On the other hand, I judge those rulers to be dependent on the support of others who could not take the field against any potential enemy, but would be obliged to take shelter behind the walls of their cities and castles, and stay there. We have talked already about those who can look after themselves, and we will have more to say in due course; to those who are in the second situation, all one can do is advise them to build defenseworks and stockpile arms, and to give up all thought of holding the open ground. He who has well fortified his city and who has followed the policies towards his own subjects that I have outlined above and will describe below, can be sure his enemies will think twice before they attack him, for people are always reluctant to undertake enterprises that look as if they will be difficult, and no one thinks it will be easy to attack someone who is well-fortified and has the support of the populace.

The cities of Germany are free to do as they please. They have little surrounding territory, and obey the emperor only when they want. They fear neither him nor any other ruler in their region, for they are so well-fortified everyone thinks it will be tedious and difficult to take them. They all have appropriate moats and ramparts, and enough artillery. They always keep in the public stores enough and drink, and enough firewood, to be able to hold out for a year. Moreover, in order to be able to keep the populace quiet and to guarantee tax revenues, they always keep in stock enough supplies to keep their subjects occupied for a year in those crafts that are the basis of the city's prosperity and provide employment for the bulk of the people. They also emphasize military preparedness and have numerous ordinances designed to ensure this.

A ruler, therefore, who has a well-fortified city, and who does not set out to make enemies, is not going to be attacked; and, suppose someone does attack him, his adversary will have to give up in disgrace. For political circumstances change so fast it is impossible for anyone to keep an army in the field for a year doing nothing but maintaining a siege. And if you are tempted to reply that if the people have property outside the city walls and see it burning, then they will not be able patiently to withstand a siege, and that as time goes by, and their own interests are damaged, they will forget their loyalty to their ruler; then I reply that a ruler who is strong and bold will always be able to overcome such difficulties, sometimes encouraging his subjects to think relief is at hand, sometimes terrifying them with stories of what the enemy will do to them if they concede defeat, sometimes taking appropriate action to neutralize those who seem to him to be agitators. Moreover, it is in the nature of things that the enemy will burn and pillage the countryside when they first arrive, at which time the subjects will still be feeling brave and prepared to undertake their own defense. So the ruler has little to fear, for after a few days, when the subjects are feeling less courageous, the damage will already have been done, and it will be too late to prevent it. Then they will be all the more ready to rally to their ruler, believing him to be in their debt, since they have had their houses burnt and their possessions looted for defending him. It is in men's nature to feel as obliged by the good they do to others, as by the good others do to them. So if you consider all the factors, you will see it is not difficult for a wise ruler to keep his subjects loyal during a siege, both at the beginning and as it continues, providing they are not short of food and of arms.

Chapter Eleven: About ecclesiastical states.

All that remains for us to discuss, at this point, is the ecclesiastical states. As far as they are concerned, all the problems are encountered before one gets possession of them. One acquires them either through strength [*virtù*] or through luck, but one can hold on to them without either. For they are maintained by their long-established institutions that are rooted in religion. These have developed to such a pitch of strength they can support their rulers in power no matter how they live and behave. Only ecclesiastical rulers have states, but no need to defend them; subjects, but no need to govern them. Their states, though they do not defend them, are not taken from them; their subjects, though they do not govern them, do not resent them, and they neither think of replacing their rulers nor are they in a position to do so. So these are the only rulers who are secure and happy. But because they are ruled by a higher power, which human intelligence cannot grasp, I will say no more about them; for, since they have been built up and maintained by God, only a presumptuous and rash person would debate about them. Nevertheless, if someone were to ask me how it comes about that the church has acquired so much temporal power, given that, until the papacy of Alexander [VI], the rulers of Italy, and indeed not only those who called themselves rulers, but every baron and lord, no matter how small, regarded the papacy's temporal power as of little significance, while now a King of France trembles at its power, for a pope has kicked him out of Italy and been the ruin of the Venetians: Though the answer to this question is well known, I think it will not be a waste of time to remind you of the main principles.

Before Charles, King of France, invaded Italy, control over this geographical region was divided between the pope, the Republic of Venice, the King of Naples, the Duke of Milan, and the Republic of Florence.[42] These rulers were obliged to have two principal preoccupations: In the first place, they had to make sure no foreign power brought an army into Italy; in the second, they had to make sure none of the Italian powers increased its territory. The powers they were most concerned about were the pope and the Venetians. In order to prevent the Venetians from expanding all the rest had to cooperate, as happened when the Venetians tried to take Ferrara.[43] In order to keep the pope in his place they relied on the nobles of Rome. These were divided into two factions, the Orsini and the Colonna, and so there was always occasion for friction between them. Because both factions were constantly in arms within sight of the pope, their strength kept the pope weak and sickly. Although there was occasionally a pope who had ambitions, Sixtus [IV] for example, yet neither luck nor skill enabled him to free himself of that handicap.

42. Charles VIII invaded Italy in 1494.
43. In 1482–84.

The real cause was the shortness of the popes' lives. On average, a pope lived ten years, which was scarcely enough time to crush one of the factions. Suppose a pope had almost destroyed the Colonna; his successor would prove to be an enemy of the Orsini, would rebuild the power of the Colonna, and would not have time to crush the Orsini. The result was the temporal power of the pope was not thought by the Italians to be of much importance. Then along came Alexander VI, who, more than all the other popes there have been, demonstrated how much a pope, using both money and arms, could get his own way. It was Alexander who, by making use of Duke Valentino and by taking advantage of the invasion of Italy by the French, brought about all those things I have mentioned above, when discussing the achievements of the duke.[44] Although his objective was not to make the church, but rather the duke, powerful, nevertheless, he did make the church a power to be reckoned with. It was the church that, after he had died and the duke had been destroyed, inherited the results of his labors.

After him came Julius [II]. The church was already powerful, for it had control of the whole of the Romagna, and the barons of Rome had been crushed, and the two factions of Orsini and Colonna had, as a result of the hiding given them by Alexander, been eliminated. Moreover, Julius had opportunities to accumulate money of a sort that had not existed before Alexander. Julius not only took over where Alexander had left off, but made further advances. He planned to acquire Bologna, to destroy the power of the Venetians, and to throw the French out of Italy. He not only laid plans, but he succeeded in everything he undertook. His achievements were all the more admirable in that his goal was to build up the power of the Church, not of any private individual. He kept the factions of the Orsini and the Colonna in the feeble condition in which he had found them. Although they made some efforts to rise again, two things kept them down: in the first place, the new power of the church, which intimidated them; and in the second, the fact none of their number were cardinals, for it is the cardinals who have been at the origin of the conflicts between the factions. These two factions have never behaved themselves at times when they have had cardinals, for the cardinals, both in Rome and outside Rome, foster the factions, and the barons are obliged to come to their support. Thus the ambition of the prelates is the cause of the conflicts and tumults among the nobility.

Now His Holiness Pope Leo [X] has acquired the papacy, along with all its immense temporal power. We may hope, if his predecessors

44. See chapter seven.

made it a military power to be reckoned with, he, who is so good and has so many virtues [*virtù*], will not only increase its power, but also make it worthy of respect.

Chapter Twelve: How many types of army are there, and what opinion should one have of mercenary soldiers?

So far I have discussed one by one the various types of one-man rule I listed at the beginning, and I have to some extent described the policies that make each type succeed or fail. I have shown the various techniques employed by numerous individuals who have sought to acquire and to hold on to power. Now my task is to outline the various strategies for offense and defense that are common to all these principalities. I said above it was necessary for a ruler to lay good foundations; otherwise, he is likely to be destroyed. The principal foundations on which the power of all governments is based (whether they be new, long-established, or mixed) are good laws and good armies. And, since there cannot be good laws where there are not good armies, and since where there are good armies, there must be good laws, I will omit any discussion of laws, and will talk about armies.

Let me begin by saying, then, that a ruler defends his state with armies that are made up of his own subjects, or of mercenaries, or of auxiliary forces, or of some combination of these three types. Mercenaries and auxiliaries are both useless and dangerous. Anyone who relies on mercenary troops to keep himself in power will never be safe or secure, for they are factious, ambitious, ill-disciplined, treacherous. They show off to your allies and run away from your enemies. They do not fear God and do not keep faith with mankind. A mercenary army puts off defeat for only so long as it postpones going into battle. In peacetime they pillage you, in wartime they let the enemy do it. This is why: They have no motive or principle for joining up beyond the desire to collect their pay. And what you pay them is not enough to make them want to die for you. They are delighted to be your soldiers when you are not at war; when you are at war, they walk away when they do not run. It should not be difficult to convince you of this, because the sole cause of the present ruin of Italy has been the fact that for many years now the Italians have been willing to rely on mercenaries. It is true that occasionally a ruler seems to benefit from their use, and they boast of their own prowess, but as soon as they face foreign troops their true worth becomes apparent. This is why Charles, King of France, was able to conquer Italy with a piece of chalk; and the person who said we were being punished for our sins spoke the truth.[45] But our sins were not the ones of which he was thinking, but those I have been discussing. Because these were the sins of our rulers, our rulers as well as the common people had to pay the price for them.

I want now to make crystal clear the worthlessness of mercenary armies. Mercenary commanders are either excellent or not. If they are excellent, you cannot trust them, for they will always be looking for ways of increasing their own power, either by turning on you, their employer, or by turning on others whom you want them to leave alone. On the other hand, if they are not first rate [*virtuoso*], then they will be the ruin of you in the normal course of events. And if you want to reply the same problems will arise whoever makes up the army, whether they are mercenaries or not, I will argue it depends on whether they take their orders from a sovereign or from a republic. A sovereign ought to go to war himself, and be his own general. A republic has to send one of its citizens. If it chooses someone who turns out not to be a successful soldier, it must replace him; if it chooses someone who is successful, it must tie his hands with laws, to ensure he keeps within the limits assigned to him. Experience shows individual sovereigns and republics that arm the masses are capable of making vast conquests; but mercenary troops are always a liability. Moreover, it is harder for a treacherous citizen to suborn an army consisting of his own fellow subjects than one made up of foreigners.

Rome and Sparta were armed and free for many centuries. The Swiss are armed to the teeth and do not have to take orders from anyone. In ancient history, we can take the Carthaginians as an example of the consequences of relying on mercenaries. They were in danger of being oppressed by their mercenary soldiers when the first war with Rome was over,[46] despite the fact they employed their own citizens as commanders. Philip of Macedon was made general of the Theban armies after the death of Epaminondas; and, after he had won the war, he enslaved the Thebans.[47] In modern times, Milan, after Duke Filippo died, employed Francesco Sforza to fight the Venetians. Once he had defeated the enemy at Caravaggio, he joined forces with them to attack the Milanese, his employers.[48] Sforza his father, who was employed

---

45. The chalk was used by Charles's quartermasters to mark the soldiers' billets. Savonarola attributed Charles's victory to sins such as fornication and usury.

46. In 346 B.C.

47. In 338 B.C.

48. In 1448.

by Queen Giovanna of Naples, abandoned her without warning and without defenses.[49] As a consequence, she was obliged to throw herself into the embrace of the King of Aragon in order to hold on to her kingdom. If the Venetians and the Florentines have in the past succeeded in acquiring new territory with mercenary armies, and if their commanders have not seized the conquests for themselves, but have held onto them for their employers, this, I would argue, is because the Florentines have had more than their share of luck. For of the first-rate [*virtuosi*] commanders, whom they would have had reason to fear, some have not been victorious, some have not been in sole command, and some have turned their ambitions elsewhere. It was John Hawkwood who did not win: We cannot know if he would have proved reliable had he been victorious, but no one can deny that if he had won Florence would have been his for the taking.[50] Sforza always had to share command with the Braccheschi, and neither could act for fear of the other. Francesco turned his ambitions to Lombardy; Braccio[51] turned his against the church and the Kingdom of Naples.

But let us look at what happened only a short time ago. The Florentines made Paolo Vitelli their commander.[52] He was a very astute man, and, despite being of modest origin, he had acquired a tremendous reputation. If he had succeeded in taking Pisa, no one can deny the Florentines would have needed his goodwill, for, if he had transferred his support to their enemies, they would have been without defenses; and if they had managed to keep his support, they would have had no choice but to do as he told them.

Consider next the conquests made by the Venetians. You will see they ran no risks and won magnificent victories as long as they relied on their own troops, which was until they tried to conquer territory on the mainland. When they armed both the nobility and the populace they had a magnificent fighting force [*operorono virtuosissimamente*], but when they began to fight on the mainland they abandoned this sound policy [*questa virtù*], and began to copy the other Italian states. When they began their conquests on the mainland, because they had little territory there, and because their own reputation was fearsome, they had little to fear from their mercenary commanders. But as their conquests extended, as they did under Carmagnola, they began to discover

49. In 1420.
50. Hawkwood (ca. 1320–94) began to be employed by Florence in 1380.
51. Andrea Fortebraccio (1368–1424).
52. In 1498.

their mistake.[53] They recognized he was a first-rate [*virtuosissimo*] general, and that they had, under his command, defeated the Duke of Milan, but they realized he had lost his taste for war, and concluded they could no longer win with him, because he no longer wanted victory; but they could not dismiss him, or the land they had acquired would go with him. So, in order to neutralize him, they had to kill him. Since then they have employed as commanders of their forces Bartolemeo of Bergamo, Roberto of San Severino, the Count of Pitigliano, and others like them. With such commanders they had reason to fear defeat, not the consequences of victory. And indeed they were defeated at Vailà, where, in one day, they lost all they had acquired with so much effort in eight hundred years.[54] For with mercenary troops one acquires new territory slowly, feebly, after many attempts; but one loses so much so quickly that it seems an act of God.

And, since these examples have been drawn from recent Italian experience, and since Italy has been entirely dependent on mercenary forces for many years, I want to trace the present state of affairs back to its source, so that, having seen the origin and development of the problem, it will be easier to see how to correct it. You need to understand, then, that in modern times, as soon as the authority of the Holy Roman Empire began to be rejected in Italy, and the pope began to acquire greater authority in temporal affairs, Italy began to be divided into a number of different states. Many of the larger cities went to war against the nobility of the surrounding countryside, who had been oppressing them, and who were, at first, supported by the emperor. The Church, on the other hand, favored the cities in order to build up its temporal authority. In many other cities individual citizens established princedoms. So Italy came to be more or less divided up between those who owed allegiance to the papacy and a number of independent republican city states. Since neither the priests nor the citizens of the republics were accustomed to fighting wars, they began to employ foreigners in their armies.

The first to win a reputation for these mercenary troops was Alberigo of Conio in the Romagna.[55] Among those who were trained by him were Braccio and Sforza, who were, at the height of their powers, the

---

53. Francesco Bussone, Count of Carmagnola (b. ca. 1390), hired by the Venetians in 1425, executed in 1432.

54. The Battle of Vailà, generally known as Agnadello, 4 May 1509.

55. Really the first Italian: He had been preceded, for example, by Hawkwood. He was victor at Marino (1379) and died in 1409.

arbiters of Italian affairs. After them came all the others who have commanded mercenary forces down to the present time. The outcome of all their prowess [*virtù*] has been that Italy has, in quick succession, been overrun by Charles, plundered by Louis, raped by Ferdinand, and humiliated by the Swiss.

The first objective these mercenary commanders have pursued has been to destroy the reputation of the infantry in order to build up that of their own forces. They did this because they have had no resources of their own, but have been dependent on their contracts. A few infantry would have done little for their reputation, while they could not afford to feed a large number. So they specialized in cavalry, for they could feed a reasonably large number, and with them win respect. It came to the point that in an army of twenty thousand soldiers there would not even be two thousand infantry. In addition, they have done everything they could to free themselves and their troops from trouble and from danger. During skirmishes between opposing forces they did not kill each other: Indeed, they not only took prisoners, but released them without demanding a ransom. They were in no hurry to assault fortifications under cover of darkness, while the defending troops were far from eager to mount sorties against their assailants. When they made camp they did not protect themselves with trenches or palisades. They passed the winters in barracks. And all these practices were permitted by their standing orders and were invented, as I said, so they could avoid effort and risk: so much so that they have reduced Italy to a despicable slavery.

Chapter Thirteen: About auxiliary troops, native troops, and
                            composite armies.

Auxiliaries are the other sort of useless troops. You rely on auxiliaries when you appeal to another ruler to come with his own armies to assist or defend you. This is what Pope Julius did in recent times, when, having discovered the incompetence of his mercenary troops during the siege of Ferrara, he decided to rely on auxiliaries, and reached an agreement with King Ferdinand of Spain that he would come to his assistance with his men and arms.[56] Auxiliary troops can be useful and good when fighting on their own behalf, but they are almost always a liability for anyone relying on their assistance. For if they lose, it is you who are defeated; if they win, you are their prisoner. There are plenty of examples of this in ancient history, but I do not want to stray

56. In 1510.

from the contemporary case of Pope Julius II; he can have had no idea what he was doing when, in the hope of acquiring Ferrara, he placed himself entirely into the hands of a foreigner. But he was lucky: The outcome was neither defeat nor imprisonment, so he did not have to pay the price for his foolish decision. His auxiliaries were routed at Ravenna,[57] but then the Swiss came along and drove out the victors, so that, contrary to everyone's expectation, including his own, he did not end up either a prisoner of his enemies, who had fled, or of his auxiliaries, for it was not they who had been victorious. Another example: The Florentines, having no troops of their own, brought ten thousand French soldiers to take Pisa.[58] This decision placed them in more danger than at any other time during their troubles. Again, the Emperor of Constantinople, in order to attack his neighbors, brought ten thousand Turks into Greece. They, when the war was over, had no intention of leaving: This was the beginning of Greece's enslavement to the infidels.[59]

He, then, who has no desire to be the victor should use these troops, for they are much more dangerous than mercenaries. If your auxiliaries win you are ruined, for they are united in their obedience to someone else. If your mercenaries win it takes them more time and more favorable circumstances to turn against you, for they are not united among themselves, and it is you who recruited and paid them. If you appoint an outsider to command them, it takes him time to establish sufficient authority to be able to attack you. In short, where mercenaries are concerned the main risk is cowardice; with auxiliaries it is valor [*virtù*].

A wise ruler, therefore, will always avoid using mercenary and auxiliary troops, and will rely on his own forces. He would rather lose with his own troops than win with someone else's, for he will not regard it a true victory if it is won with troops that do not belong to him. I never hesitate to cite Cesare Borgia as a model to be imitated. This duke entered the Romagna with an auxiliary army, for his troops were all Frenchmen, and he used it to take Imola and Forlì.[60] But since he did not feel such troops were reliable, he then switched over to mercenaries, believing that using them involved fewer risks, and so he hired the Orsini and the Vitelli. But in practice he found them unreliable, treacherous, and dangerous, and so he got rid of them and formed his own

57. 11 April 1512.
58. In 1500.
59. The war lasted from 1341 to 1347; Constantinople did not finally fall to the Turks until 1453.
60. In the winter of 1499–1500.

army. And it is easy to see the differences among these three types of army, for you only have to consider how the duke's reputation changed, depending on whether he was relying on the French alone, on the Orsini and the Vitelli, or on his own troops and his own resources. With each change of policy it increased, but he was taken seriously only when everyone could see he was in complete command of his own forces.

I wanted to stick to examples that are both recent and Italian, but I cannot resist mentioning Hiero of Syracuse, since I have already discussed him above. He, when he was made commander-in-chief by the Syracusans, as I have described, quickly realized their mercenary army was worthless, for it was made up of condottieri like our own Italian armies. He decided he could not risk either keeping them on, or letting them go, so he had them massacred. Thereafter, he went to war with troops of his own, not with other people's soldiers. I also want to remind you of an Old Testament story that is relevant. When David proposed to Saul that he should go and fight with Goliath, the Philistine champion, Saul, in order to give him confidence, dressed him in his own armor. David, having tried it on, rejected it, saying he could not give a good account of himself if he relied on Saul's weapons. He wanted to confront the enemy armed with his sling and his knife.[61]

In short, someone else's armor either falls off, or it weighs you down, or it trips you up. Charles VII, father of King Louis XI, having through good luck and valor [*virtù*] driven the English out of France,[62] recognized that it was essential to have one's own weapons and, so, issued instructions for the establishment of a standing army of cavalry and infantry. Later, his son King Louis abolished the infantry[63] and began to recruit Swiss troops. It was this mistake, imitated by his successors, that was, as we can see from recent events, the cause of the dangers faced by that kingdom.[64] For he built up the reputation of the Swiss while undermining his own military capacity, for he destroyed his own infantry and made his own cavalry dependent on the support of foreign troops, for they, having become accustomed to fighting alongside the Swiss, no longer think they can win without them. The result is the French dare not fight against the Swiss, and without the Swiss they are ineffective against anyone else. So the French armies have been

61. I Kings 17.

62. In 1453.

63. In 1474.

64. Machiavelli is thinking of the defeats of 1512, which had virtually forced the French out of Italy.

mixed, partly mercenary and partly native. Such a mixed army is much preferable to one made up only of auxiliaries or only of mercenaries, but it is much inferior to one made up entirely of one's own troops. The French example is sufficient to make the point, for the Kingdom of France would be able to overcome any enemy if the foundations laid by Charles VII had been built upon, or even if his instructions had merely been kept in force. But men are foolish, and they embark on something that is attractive in its outward appearance, without recognizing the evil consequences that will follow from it: a point I have already made when talking about consumption.

A ruler who cannot foresee evil consequences before they have time to develop is not truly wise; but few have such wisdom. And if one studies the first destruction of the Roman Empire one discovers it came about as a result of the first recruitment of Gothic soldiers,[65] for from that moment the armies of the Roman Empire began to grow feeble. And all the strength [*virtù*] that ebbed from the Romans accrued to the Goths. I conclude, therefore, that no ruler is secure unless he has his own troops. Without them he is entirely dependent on fortune, having no strength [*virtù*] with which to defend himself in adversity. Wise men have always believed and said that, "Nothing is so fragile as a reputation for strength that does not correspond to one's real capacities." Now one's own troops can be made up out of one's subjects, or one's citizens, or one's dependents: All others are either mercenaries or auxiliaries. And the correct way of organizing one's own troops is easy to find out by looking over the instructions given by the four rulers whose conduct I have approved, or by finding out how Philip, the father of Alexander the Great, and how many other republics and sovereigns levied and trained troops: I have complete confidence in their methods.

Chapter Fourteen: What a ruler should do as regards the militia.

A ruler, then, should have no other concern, no other thought, should pay attention to nothing aside from war, military institutions, and the training of his soldiers. For this is the only field in which a ruler has to excel. It is of such importance [*virtù*] that military prowess not only keeps those who have been born rulers in power, but also often enables men who have been born private citizens to come to power. On the other hand, one sees that when rulers think more about luxuries than about weapons, they fall from power. The prime reason for losing

65. In 376.

power is neglect of military matters; while being an expert soldier opens the way to the acquisition of power.

Francesco Sforza, because he had troops, became Duke of Milan,[66] having begun life as a private citizen. His descendants, who had no taste for the sweat and dust of a soldier's life, started out as dukes and ended up as private citizens. For, among the other deleterious consequences of not having one's own troops, one comes to be regarded with contempt. There are several types of disgrace a ruler should avoid, as I will explain below. This is one of them. For there is no comparison between a ruler who has his own troops and one who has not. It is not to be expected that someone who is armed should cheerfully obey someone who is defenseless, or that someone who has no weapon should be safe when his employees are armed. For the armed man has contempt for the man without weapons; the defenseless man does not trust someone who can overpower him. The two cannot get on together. So, too, a ruler who does not know how to organize a militia, beyond the other dangers he faces, which I have already described, must recognize that he will not be respected by his troops, and that he cannot trust them.

So a ruler must think only of military matters, and in time of peace he should be even more occupied with them than in time of war. There are two ways he can prepare for war: by thinking and by doing. As far as actions are concerned, he should not only keep his troops in good order and see they are well-trained; he should be always out hunting, thereby accustoming his body to fatigue. He should take the opportunity to study the lie of the land, climbing the mountains, descending into the valleys, crossing the plains, fording rivers, and wading through marshes. He should spare no effort to become acquainted with his own land, and this for two reasons. First, the knowledge will stand him in good stead if he has to defend his state against invasion; second, his knowledge and experience on his own terrain will make it easy for him to understand any other landscape with which he has to become acquainted from scratch. The hills, the valleys, the plains, the rivers, the marshes of, for example, Tuscany have a good deal in common with those of the other regions of Italy. A knowledge of the terrain in one region will make it easy for him to learn about the others. A ruler who lacks this sort of skill does not satisfy the first requirement in a military commander, for it is knowledge of the terrain that enables you to locate the enemy and to get the edge over him when deciding where

66. In 1450.

to camp, in what order to march, how to draw up the troops on the field of battle, and where to build fortifications.

Philopoemon,[67] ruler of the Achaeans, is much praised by the historians,[68] but in particular he is admired because during peacetime he thought about nothing but warfare. When he was out riding in the countryside with his friends, he would often halt and ask: "If the enemy were up on those hills, and we were down here with our army, who would have the better position? How should we advance, following the rule book, to attack him? If we wanted to retreat, how would we set about it? If they were retreating, how would we pursue them?" And so he would invite them to discuss, as they rode along, all the possible eventualities an army may have to face. He listened to their views, he explained his own and backed them up with arguments. Thanks to this continual theorizing he ensured that, if he was at the head of an army, he would be perfectly prepared for anything that might happen.

Such theorizing is not enough. Every ruler should read history books, and in them he should study the actions of admirable men. He should see how they conducted themselves when at war, study why they won some battles and lost others, so he will know what to imitate and what to avoid. Above all he should set himself to imitate the actions of some admirable historical character, as great men have always imitated their glorious predecessors, constantly bearing in mind their actions and their ways of behaving. So, it is said, Alexander the Great took Achilles as his model; Caesar took Alexander; Scipio took Cyrus. If you read the life of Cyrus that was written by Xenophon and then study the life of Scipio you will realize to what extent those qualities that are admired in Scipio derive from Cyrus: His chastity, his affability, his kindness, his generosity, all are modelled upon Cyrus as Xenophon portrays him. A wise ruler will follow these examples. He will never relax during peacetime, but will always be working to take advantage of the opportunities peace presents, so he will be fully prepared when adversity comes. When his luck changes, he must be ready to fight back.

Chapter Fifteen: About those factors that cause men, and especially rulers, to be praised or censured.

Our next task is to consider the policies and principles a ruler ought to follow in dealing with his subjects or with his friends. Since I know

67. 253–184 B.C.
68. Livy, bk. 25, ch. 28. Machiavelli would also have known the accounts in Plutarch and Polybius.

many people have written on this subject, I am concerned it may be thought presumptuous for me to write on it as well, especially since what I have to say, as regards this question in particular, will differ greatly from the recommendations of others.[69] But my hope is to write a book that will be useful, at least to those who read it intelligently, and so I thought it sensible to go straight to a discussion of how things are in real life and not waste time with a discussion of an imaginary world. For many authors have constructed imaginary republics and principalities that have never existed in practice and never could; for the gap between how people actually behave and how they ought to behave is so great that anyone who ignores everyday reality in order to live up to an ideal will soon discover he has been taught how to destroy himself, not how to preserve himself. For anyone who wants to act the part of a good man in all circumstances will bring about his own ruin, for those he has to deal with will not all be good. So it is necessary for a ruler, if he wants to hold on to power, to learn how not to be good, and to know when it is and when it is not necessary to use this knowledge.

Let us leave to one side, then, all discussion of imaginary rulers and talk about practical realities. I maintain that all men, when people talk about them, and especially rulers, because they hold positions of authority, are described in terms of qualities that are inextricably linked to censure or to praise. So one man is described as generous, another as a miser [*misero*] (to use the Tuscan term; for "avaricious," in our language, is used of someone who has a rapacious desire to acquire wealth, while we call someone a "miser" when he is unduly reluctant to spend the money he has); one is called open-handed, another tight-fisted; one man is cruel, another gentle; one untrustworthy, another reliable; one effeminate and cowardly, another bold and violent; one sympathetic, another self-important; one promiscuous, another monogamous; one straightforward, another duplicitous; one tough, another easy-going; one serious, another cheerful; one religious, another atheistical; and so on. Now I know everyone will agree that if a ruler could have all the good qualities I have listed and none of the bad ones, then this would be an excellent state of affairs. But one cannot have all the good qualities, nor always act in a praiseworthy fashion, for we do not live in an ideal world. You have to be astute enough to avoid being thought to have those evil qualities that would make it impossible for you to retain power; as for those that are compati-

---

69. Machiavelli is thinking in particular of Cicero, *De officiis*, and Seneca, *De clementia*.

ble with holding on to power, you should avoid them if you can; but if you cannot, then you should not worry too much if people say you have them. Above all, do not be upset if you are supposed to have those vices a ruler needs if he is going to stay securely in power, for, if you think about it, you will realize there are some ways of behaving that are supposed to be virtuous [*che parrà virtù*], but would lead to your downfall, and others that are supposed to be wicked, but will lead to your welfare and peace of mind.

Chapter Sixteen: On generosity and parsimony.

Let me begin, then, with the qualities I mentioned first. I argue it would be good to be thought generous; nevertheless, if you act in the way that will get you a reputation for generosity, you will do yourself damage. For generosity used skillfully [*virtuosamente*] and practiced as it ought to be, is hidden from sight, and being truly generous will not protect you from acquiring a reputation for parsimony. So, if you want to have a reputation for generosity, you must throw yourself into lavish and ostentatious expenditure. Consequently, a ruler who pursues a reputation for generosity will always end up wasting all his resources; and he will be obliged in the end, if he wants to preserve his reputation, to impose crushing taxes upon the people, to pursue every possible source of income, and to be preoccupied with maximizing his revenues. This will begin to make him hateful to his subjects, and will ensure no one thinks well of him, for no one admires poverty. The result is his supposed generosity will have caused him to offend the vast majority and to have won favor with few. Anything that goes wrong will destabilize him, and the slightest danger will imperil him. Recognizing the problem, and trying to economize, he will quickly find he has acquired a reputation as a miser.

So we see a ruler cannot seek to benefit from a reputation as generous [*questa virtù del liberale*] without harming himself. Recognizing this, he ought, if he is wise, not to mind being called miserly. For, as time goes by, he will be thought of as growing ever more generous, for people will recognize that as a result of his parsimony he is able to live on his income, maintain an adequate army, and undertake new initiatives without imposing new taxes. The result is he will be thought to be generous towards all those whose income he does not tax, which is almost everybody, and stingy towards those who miss out on handouts, who are only a few. In modern times nobody has succeeded on a large scale except those who have been thought miserly; the others came to nothing. Pope Julius II took advantage of a reputation for generosity in order to win election, but once elected he made no effort to keep his reputation, for he wanted to go to war. The present King of France[70] has fought many wars without having to impose additional taxes on his people, because his occasional additional expenditures are offset by his long-term parsimony. The present King of Spain[71] could not have aspired to, or achieved, so many conquests if he had had a reputation for generosity.

So a ruler should not care about being thought miserly, for it means he will be able to avoid robbing his subjects; he will be able to defend himself; he will not become poor and despicable, and he will not be forced to become rapacious. This is one of those vices that make successful government possible. And if you say: But Caesar rose to power thanks to his generosity, and many others have made their way to the highest positions of authority because they have both been and have been thought to be generous. I reply, either you are already a ruler, or you are on your way to becoming one. If you are already a ruler, generosity is a mistake; if you are trying to become one then you do, indeed, need to be thought of as generous. Caesar was one of those competing to become the ruler of Rome; but if, having acquired power, he had lived longer and had not learned to reduce his expenditures, he would have destroyed his own position. You may be tempted to reply: Many established rulers who have been thought to be immensely generous have been successful in war. But my answer is: Rulers either spend their own wealth and that of their subjects, or that of other people. Those who spend their own and their subjects' wealth should be abstemious; those who spend the wealth of others should seize every opportunity to be generous. Rulers who march with their armies, living off plunder, pillage, and confiscations are spending other people's money, and it is essential they should seem generous, for otherwise their soldiers will not follow them. With goods that belong neither to you nor to your subjects, you can afford to be generous, as Cyrus, Caesar, and Alexander were. Squandering other people's money does not do your reputation any harm, quite the reverse. The problem is with squandering your own. There is nothing so self-defeating as generosity, for the more generous you are, the less you are able to be generous. Generosity leads to poverty and disgrace, or, if you try to escape that, to rapacity and hostility. Among all the things a ruler should try to avoid, he must avoid above all being hated and despised. Generosity leads to your being both. So it is wiser to accept a reputation

70. Louis XII.
71. Ferdinand the Catholic.

as miserly, which people despise but do not hate, than to aspire to a reputation as generous, and as a consequence, be obliged to face criticism for rapacity, which people both despise and hate.

Chapter Seventeen: About cruelty and compassion; and about whether it is better to be loved than feared, or the reverse.

Going further down our list of qualities, I recognize every ruler should want to be thought of as compassionate and not cruel. Nevertheless, I have to warn you to be careful about being compassionate. Cesare Borgia was thought of as cruel; but this supposed cruelty of his restored order to the Romagna, united it, rendered it peaceful and law-abiding. If you think about it, you will realize he was, in fact, much more compassionate than the people of Florence, who, in order to avoid being thought cruel, allowed Pistoia to tear itself apart.[72] So a ruler ought not to mind the disgrace of being called cruel, if he keeps his subjects peaceful and law-abiding, for it is more compassionate to impose harsh punishments on a few than, out of excessive compassion, to allow disorder to spread, which leads to murders or looting. The whole community suffers if there are riots, while to maintain order the ruler only has to execute one or two individuals. Of all rulers, he who is new to power cannot escape a reputation for cruelty, for he is surrounded by dangers. Virgil has Dido say:

> Harsh necessity, and the fact my kingdom is new, oblige me to do
> these things,
> And to mass my armies on the frontiers.[73]

Nevertheless, you should be careful how you assess the situation and should think twice before you act. Do not be afraid of your own shadow. Employ policies that are moderated by prudence and sympathy. Avoid excessive self-confidence, which leads to carelessness, and avoid excessive timidity, which will make you insupportable.

This leads us to a question that is in dispute: Is it better to be loved than feared, or vice versa?[74] My reply is one ought to be both loved and feared; but, since it is difficult to accomplish both at the same time, I maintain it is much safer to be feared than loved, if you have

72. In 1501.

73. Virgil, *Aeneid*, I, 563–4.

74. Cicero, *De officiis*, bk. 2, ch. 7, § 23–24.

to do without one of the two. For of men one can, in general, say this: They are ungrateful, fickle, deceptive and deceiving, avoiders of danger, eager to gain. As long as you serve their interests, they are devoted to you. They promise you their blood, their possessions, their lives, and their children, as I said before, so long as you seem to have no need of them. But as soon as you need help, they turn against you. Any ruler who relies simply on their promises and makes no other preparations, will be destroyed. For you will find that those whose support you buy, who do not rally to you because they admire your strength of character and nobility of soul, these are people you pay for, but they are never yours, and in the end you cannot get the benefit of your investment. Men are less nervous of offending someone who makes himself lovable, than someone who makes himself frightening. For love attaches men by ties of obligation, which, since men are wicked, they break whenever their interests are at stake. But fear restrains men because they are afraid of punishment, and this fear never leaves them. Still, a ruler should make himself feared in such a way that, if he does not inspire love, at least he does not provoke hatred. For it is perfectly possible to be feared and not hated. You will only be hated if you seize the property or the women of your subjects and citizens. Whenever you have to kill someone, make sure you have a suitable excuse and an obvious reason; but, above all else, keep your hands off other people's property; for men are quicker to forget the death of their father than the loss of their inheritance. Moreover, there are always reasons why you might want to seize people's property; and he who begins to live by plundering others will always find an excuse for seizing other people's possessions; but there are fewer reasons for killing people, and one killing need not lead to another.

When a ruler is at the head of his army and has a vast number of soldiers under his command, then it is absolutely essential to be prepared to be thought cruel; for it is impossible to keep an army united and ready for action without acquiring a reputation for cruelty. Among the extraordinary accomplishments of Hannibal, we may note one in particular: He commanded a vast army, made up of men of many different nations, who were fighting far from home, yet they never mutinied and they never fell out with one another, either when things were going badly, or when things were going well.[75] The only possible explanation for this is that he was known to be harsh and cruel. This, together with his numerous virtues [*virtù*], meant his soldiers always

75. Hannibal (247–ca. 183 B.C.) campaigned in Italy from 218 to 203 B.C. Machiavelli's source is Polybius, bk. 11, ch. 19.

regarded him with admiration and fear. Without cruelty, his other virtues [*virtù*] would not have done the job. Those who write about Hannibal without thinking things through both admire the loyalty of his troops and criticize the cruelty that was its principal cause. If you doubt my claim that his other virtues [*virtù*] would have been insufficient, take the case of Scipio.[76] He was not only unique in his own day, but history does not record anyone his equal. But his army rebelled against him in Spain.[77] The sole cause of this was his excessive leniency, which meant his soldiers had more freedom than is compatible with good military discipline. Fabius Maximus criticized him for this in the senate and accused him of corrupting the Roman armies. When Locri was destroyed by one of his commanders,[78] he did not avenge the deaths of the inhabitants, and he did not punish his officer's insubordination. He was too easygoing. This was so apparent that one of his supporters in the senate was obliged to excuse him by saying he was no different from many other men, who were better at doing their own jobs than at making other people do theirs. In course of time, had he remained in command without learning from his mistakes, this aspect of Scipio's character would have destroyed his glorious reputation. But, because his authority was subordinate to that of the senate, not only were the consequences of this defect mitigated, but it even enhanced his reputation.

I conclude, then, that, as far as being feared and loved is concerned, since men decide for themselves whom they love, and rulers decide whom they fear, a wise ruler should rely on the emotion he can control, not on the one he cannot. But he must take care to avoid being hated, as I have said.

Chapter Eighteen: How far rulers are to keep their word.

Everybody recognizes how praiseworthy it is for a ruler to keep his word and to live a life of integrity, without relying on craftiness. Nevertheless, we see that in practice, in these days, those rulers who have not thought it important to keep their word have achieved great things, and have known how to employ cunning to confuse and disorientate other men. In the end, they have been able to overcome those who have placed store in integrity.

76. Scipio (ca.236–183 B.C.) defeated Hannibal at Zama in North Africa (202 B.C.).
77. In 206 B.C. Livy, bk. 28, chs. 24–29.
78. In 205 B.C.

You should therefore know there are two ways to fight: one while respecting the rules, the other with no holds barred. Men alone fight in the first fashion, and animals fight in the second.[79] But because you cannot always win if you respect the rules, you must be prepared to break them. A ruler, in particular, needs to know how to be both an animal and a man. The classical writers, without saying it explicitly, taught rulers to behave like this. They described how Achilles, and many other rulers in ancient times, were given to Chiron the centaur to be raised, so he could bring them up as he thought best. What they intended to convey, with this story of rulers' being educated by someone who was half beast and half man, was that it is necessary for a ruler to know when to act like an animal and when like a man; and if he relies on just one or the other mode of behavior he cannot hope to survive.

Since a ruler, then, needs to know how to make good use of beastly qualities, he should take as his models among the animals both the fox and the lion, for the lion does not know how to avoid traps, and the fox is easily overpowered by wolves.[80] So you must be a fox when it comes to suspecting a trap, and a lion when it comes to making the wolves turn tail. Those who simply act like a lion all the time do not understand their business. So you see a wise ruler cannot, and should not, keep his word when doing so is to his disadvantage, and when the reasons that led him to promise to do so no longer apply. Of course, if all men were good, this advice would be bad; but since men are wicked and will not keep faith with you, you need not keep faith with them. Nor is a ruler ever short of legitimate reasons to justify breaking his word. I could give an infinite number of contemporary examples to support my argument and to show how treaties and promises have been rendered null and void by the dishonesty of rulers; and he who has known best how to act the fox has come out of it the best. But it is essential to know how to conceal how crafty one is, to know how to be a clever counterfeit and hypocrite. You will find people are so simple-minded and so preoccupied with their immediate concerns, that if you set out to deceive them, you will always find plenty of them who will let themselves be deceived.

Among the numerous recent cases one could mention, there is one of particular interest. Alexander VI had only one purpose, only one thought, which was to take people in, and he always found people who were willing victims. There never has been anyone who was more convincing when he swore an oath, nor has there been anybody who

---

79. Cicero, *De officiis*, bk. 1, ch. 11, § 34.
80. The fox and the lion are from Cicero, *De officiis*, bk. 1, ch. 13, § 41.

has ever formulated more eloquent oaths and has at the same time been quicker to break them. Nevertheless, he was able to find gulls one after another, whenever he wanted them, for he was a master of this particular skill.

So a ruler need not have all the positive qualities I listed earlier, but he must seem to have them. Indeed, I would go so far as to say that if you have them and never make any exceptions, then you will suffer for it; while if you merely appear to have them, they will benefit you. So you should seem to be compassionate, trustworthy, sympathetic, honest, religious, and, indeed, be all these things; but at the same time you should be constantly prepared, so that, if these become liabilities, you are trained and ready to become their opposites. You need to understand this: A ruler, and particularly a ruler who is new to power, cannot conform to all those rules that men who are thought good are expected to respect, for he is often obliged, in order to hold on to power, to break his word, to be uncharitable, inhumane, and irreligious. So he must be mentally prepared to act as circumstances and changes in fortune require. As I have said, he should do what is right if he can; but he must be prepared to do wrong if necessary.

A ruler must, therefore, take great care that he never carelessly says anything that is not imbued with the five qualities I listed above. He must seem, to those who listen to him and watch him, entirely pious, truthful, reliable, sympathetic, and religious. There is no quality that it is more important he should seem to have than this last one. In general, men judge more by sight than by touch. Everyone sees what is happening, but not everyone feels the consequences. Everyone sees what you seem to be; few have direct experience of who you really are. Those few will not dare speak out in the face of public opinion when that opinion is reinforced by the authority of the state. In the behavior of all men, and particularly of rulers, against whom there is no recourse at law, people judge by the outcome. So if a ruler wins wars and holds on to power, the means he has employed will always be judged honorable, and everyone will praise them. The common man accepts external appearances and judges by the outcome; and when it comes down to it only the masses count; for the elite are powerless if the masses have someone to provide them with leadership. One contemporary ruler,[81] whom it would be unwise to name, is always preaching peace and good faith, and he has not a shred of respect for either; if he had respected either one or the other, he would have lost either his state or his reputation several times by now.

81. Ferdinand the Catholic.

Chapter Nineteen: How one should avoid hatred and contempt.

Because I have spoken of the more important of the qualities I mentioned earlier, I want now to discuss the rest of them briefly under
this general heading, that a ruler must take care (I have already referred
to this in passing) to avoid those things that will make him an object
of hatred or contempt. As long as he avoids these he will have done
what is required of him, and he will find having a reputation for any
of the other vices will do him no harm at all. You become hateful,
above all, as I have said, if you prey on the possessions and the women
of your subjects. You should leave both alone. The vast majority of
men, so long as their goods and their honor are not taken from them,
will live contentedly, so you will only have to contend with the small
minority who are ambitious, and there are lots of straightforward ways
of keeping them under control. You become contemptible if you are
thought to be erratic, capricious, effeminate, pusillanimous, irresolute.
You should avoid acquiring such a reputation as a pilot steers clear of
the rocks. Make every effort to ensure your actions suggest greatness
and endurance, strength of character and of purpose. When it comes
to the private business of your subjects, you should aim to ensure you
never have to change your decisions once they have been taken, and
that you acquire a reputation that will discourage people from even
considering tricking or deceiving you.

A ruler who is thought of in these terms has the sort of reputation
he needs; and it is difficult to conspire against someone who is respected
in this way, difficult to attack him, because people realize he is on top
of his job and has the loyalty of his employees. For rulers ought to be
afraid of two things: Within the state, they should fear their subjects;
abroad, they should fear other rulers. Against foreign powers, a good
army and reliable allies are the only defense; and, if you have a good
army, you will always find your allies reliable. And you will find it easy
to maintain order at home if you are secure from external threats,
provided, that is, conspiracies against you have not undermined your
authority. Even if foreign powers do attack, if you have followed my
advice and lived according to the principles I have outlined, then, as
long as you keep a grip on yourself, you will be able to resist any attack,
just as I said Nabis of Sparta was able to. But where your subjects are
concerned, when you are not being attacked by foreign powers, you
have to be wary of secret conspiracies.[82] The best protection against

82. Influential in Machiavelli's discussion of conspiracies is Aristotle, *Politics*,
bk. 8.

these is to ensure you are not hated or despised, and the people are satisfied with your rule. It is essential to accomplish this, as I have already explained at length.

Indeed, one of the most effective defenses a ruler has against conspiracies is to make sure he is not generally hated. For conspirators always believe the assassination of the ruler will be approved by the people. If they believe the people will be angered, then they cannot screw up the courage to embark on such an enterprise, for conspirators have to overcome endless difficulties to achieve success. Experience shows the vast majority of conspiracies fail. For a conspirator cannot act alone, and he can only find associates among those whom he believes are discontented. As soon as you tell someone who is discontented what you are planning, you give him the means to satisfy his ambitions, because it is obvious he can expect to be richly rewarded if he betrays you. If he betrays you, his reward is certain; if he keeps faith with you, he faces danger, with little prospect of reward. So, you see, he needs either to be an exceptionally loyal friend or to be a completely intransigent enemy of the ruler, if he is to keep faith with you. So we can sum up as follows: The conspirators face nothing but fear, mutual distrust, and the prospect of punishment, so they lose heart; while the ruler is supported by the authority of his office and by the laws, and protected both by his supporters and by the forces of government. So, if you add to this inbuilt advantage the goodwill of the populace, then it is impossible to find anyone who is so foolhardy as to conspire against you. For in most situations a conspirator has to fear capture before he does the deed; but if the ruler has the goodwill of the people, he has to fear it afterwards as well, for the people will turn on him when the deed is done, and he will have nowhere to hide.

I could give an infinite number of examples to illustrate this, but I will confine myself to one only, a conspiracy that took place during the lifetime of our parents. Mr. Annibale Bentivoglio, grandfather of the present Mr. Annibale, was at the time ruler of Bologna. The Canneschi conspired against him and assassinated him.[83] His only surviving relative was Mr. Giovanni, who was still in the cradle. But as soon as he was killed the people rose up and killed all the Canneschi. This happened because the family of Bentivoglio had, in those days, the goodwill of the people. Their loyalty was such that, there being no surviving member of the family in Bologna who could, now Annibale was dead, take over the government, and they having heard that in Florence there was a member of the family, someone who so far had

83. In 1445.

been nothing more than the son of a blacksmith, the citizens of Bologna
came to Florence to fetch him and made him the ruler of their city.
He ruled it until Mr. Giovanni was old enough to take office.

I conclude, then, that a ruler need not worry much about conspiracies
as long as the people wish him well; but if the people are hostile to
him and hate him, then he should fear everything and everyone. States
that are well-governed and rulers who are wise make every effort to
ensure the elite are not driven to despair, and to satisfy the masses
and keep them content; for this is one of the most important tasks a
ruler must set himself.

Among the states that are well-ordered and well-ruled at the present
time is France. There you will find innumerable good institutions that
ensure the freedom of action and security of the king. First among
them is the *parlement* and its authority.[84] For whoever set up the government of that country understood the powerful are ambitious and inso-
lent, and judged it necessary they should be bridled so they could be
controlled, but on the other hand he recognized the hatred most people
have for the powerful, whom they have reason to fear, and the conse-
quent need to reassure and protect the great. So he did not want this
to be the responsibility of the king, in order to avoid his alienating the
powerful by favoring the people or alienating the people by favoring
the powerful, and he established an independent tribunal, whose task
it is, without incurring blame for the king, to crush the powerful and
defend the weak. This arrangement is as intelligent and prudent as
could be, and makes a substantial contribution to the security of the
king and the stability of the kingdom. This institution enables us to
recognize a significant general principle: Rulers should delegate responsibility for unpopular actions, while taking personal responsibility
for those that will win favor. And once again I conclude a ruler should
treat the powerful with respect, but at all costs he should avoid being
hated by the people.

Many perhaps will think, if they consider the lives and deaths of
some of the Roman emperors, that these provide examples contrary
to the opinion I have expressed. For it would seem some of them lived
exemplary lives and demonstrated great strength [*virtù*] of character,
yet they fell from power, or rather they were killed by their retainers,
who had conspired against them. Since I want to reply to this objection,
I will discuss the characters of some of the emperors, explaining the
reasons why they were destroyed, and show they do not tell against

84. The *parlement* was the highest court of appeal. Its members belonged to
a distinct social caste, the *noblesse de robe*.

my argument. This will primarily involve pointing out factors that would seem significant to anyone who read the history of those times. I will confine myself to discussing all those emperors who came after Marcus Aurelius, up to and including Maximilian:[85] that is, Marcus, his son Commodus, Pertinax, Julian, Severus, his son Antoninus Caracalla, Macrinus, Heliogabulus, Alexander, and Maximilian.

The first thing to be remarked is that, where in most states one only has to contend with the ambition of the great and the effrontery of the populace, the emperors of Rome had to face a third problem: They had to put up with the cruelty and greed of their soldiers. This was so difficult to do that it caused the downfall of many of the emperors, for it was almost impossible to satisfy both the soldiers and the populace. The people loved peace and quiet and, for this reason, liked their rulers to be unassuming; but the soldiers wanted the emperor to be a man of war and liked him to be arrogant, cruel, and rapacious. They wanted him to direct his aggression against the populace, so they could double their income and give free rein to their greed and cruelty. The result was those emperors who did not have a sufficiently intimidating reputation to keep both populace and soldiers in check (either because they did not think such a reputation desirable, or because they were incapable of acquiring it) were always destroyed. Most of them, especially those who acquired power without inheriting it, recognizing the difficulty of pleasing both soldiers and people, concentrated on pleasing the soldiers, thinking it could do little harm to alienate the populace. They had no choice, for, since rulers are bound to be hated by someone, their first concern must be to ensure they are not hated by any significant group; and, if they cannot achieve this, then they must make every possible effort to avoid the hatred of those groups that are most powerful. And so those emperors who had not inherited power and, thus, were in need of particularly strong support, attached themselves to the soldiers rather than to the people; a policy that proved successful or not, depending on whether the particular ruler in question knew how to establish his reputation with the army. For these reasons, then, Marcus, Pertinax, and Alexander, all of whom were unassuming, lovers of justice, haters of cruelty, sympathetic and kind, all came, apart from Marcus, to a tragic end. Marcus alone lived honorably and died peaceably, for he inherited power, and did not have to repay a debt to either the soldiers or the populace. Moreover, since he had many virtues [*virtù*] that made him widely respected, he was able, during his

85. In other words, the period from 161 to 238. Machiavelli follows Herodian closely, probably relying on Poliziano's Latin translation.

own lifetime, to keep both groups in their place, and he was never hated or despised. But Pertinax was made emperor against the wishes of the soldiers, who, being accustomed to an unbridled life under Commodus, were unable to tolerate the disciplined way of life Pertinax wanted to impose on them. So he made himself hated, and to this hatred was added contempt, for he was an old man, and so his rule had scarcely begun before he fell from power.

Here we should note one can become hated for the good things one does, as much as for the bad. That is why, as I said above, a ruler who wants to hold on to power is often obliged not to be good, for when some powerful group—whether the populace, the soldiers, or the elite—whose support you feel it is essential to have if you are to survive, is corrupt, then you have to adapt to its tastes in order to satisfy it, in which case doing good will do you harm. But let us turn to Alexander. He was so good that among the other things for which he is praised is the fact that during the fourteen years he retained power, nobody was ever executed at his orders without due trial. Nevertheless, he was thought effeminate, and blamed for being under the influence of his mother, and so he came to be despised, the army conspired against him and killed him.

By contrast, let us consider the qualities of Commodus, of Severus, Antoninus Caracalla, and Maximinus. They were, you will find, in the highest degree bloodthirsty and rapacious. In order to satisfy the soldiery, they did not fail to commit every possible type of crime against the populace; and all of them, with the exception of Severus, came to a bad end. For Severus was such a strong ruler [*in Severo fu tanta virtù*] that, with the support of the army, even though the populace were oppressed by him, he could always rule successfully; for his strength [*virtù*] inspired awe in the minds of both soldiers and people: The people were always to a considerable degree stupefied and astonished by him, while the soldiers were admiring and satisfied. Because his deeds were commendable in a new ruler, I want to pause to point out how well he understood how to play the part both of the fox and of the lion: These are the two styles of action I have maintained a ruler must know how to imitate. Severus, because he knew what a coward Julian the new emperor was, persuaded the army he had under his command in Slavonia that it was a good idea to march on Rome to revenge the death of Pertinax, who had been killed by his praetorian guard. With this excuse, and without displaying any ambition to seize the throne, he set out for Rome; and his army was in Italy before anyone knew it had left its station. When he reached Rome, the senate, out of fear, elected him emperor and had Julian put to death. Severus, having begun like this, faced two problems if he wanted to gain effective control of the whole empire: In Asia there was Niger, commander of the Asiatic armies, who had had himself proclaimed emperor; in the West there was Albinus, who also aspired to power. Because he thought it would be dangerous to take on both of them at once, he decided to attack Niger and deceive Albinus. So he wrote to Albinus saying now that he had been elected emperor by the senate, he wanted to share his authority with him. He offered him the title of Caesar and had the senate appoint him co-ruler. Albinus accepted these proposals at face value. But as soon as Severus had defeated and killed Niger and pacified the eastern empire, he returned to Rome and attacked Albinus in the senate, complaining that he, far from being grateful for the generosity he had been shown, had wickedly sought to assassinate him. Severus claimed to have no choice but to go and punish this ingrate. So he attacked him in France and deprived him of his offices and of his life.

Anyone who examines Severus's actions with care will find he was both a ferocious lion and a cunning fox. He will find he was feared and respected by all, and he was not hated by the armies. So it is no surprise Severus, who had not inherited power, was able to hold on to a vast empire, for his immense reputation was a constant defense against the hatred the populace might otherwise have felt for his exactions. Antoninus his son was also a man whose remarkable abilities inspired awe in the populace and gratitude in the soldiers. For he was a man of war, able to make light of the most arduous task and contemptuous of delicate food and all other luxuries. This made all his soldiers love him. Nevertheless, his ferocity and cruelty were without parallel. He did not only kill vast numbers of individuals, but, on one occasion, a large part of the population of Rome, and, on another, the whole of Alexandria. So he came to be loathed by everyone, and even his close associates began to fear him, with the result he was killed by a centurion while he was surrounded by his own troops. One should note rulers have no protection against an assassination like this, carried out by a truly determined individual, for anyone who is prepared to die can attack them. But, nevertheless, rulers should not worry unduly about such assassins because they are extremely rare. You should try merely to avoid giving grave injury to anyone you employ who comes close to you in the course of business. Antoninus had done just this, for he had outrageously put to death a brother of the centurion who killed him, and had repeatedly threatened the centurion's own life; yet he employed him as a bodyguard. This was foolhardy, and the disastrous outcome could have been predicted.

Now we come to Commodus, who had no difficulty in holding on to power, because he had inherited it, being the son of Marcus. All he had to do was follow in his father's footsteps, and he would have been satisfactory to both soldiers and populace. But, because he was by nature cruel and brutal, he began to ingratiate himself with the soldiers and to encourage them to be undisciplined, so he would be able to give his own rapacity free rein against the people. On the other hand, he did not maintain his own dignity. Often, when he went to the amphitheater, he came down and fought with the gladiators, and he did other things that were despicable and incompatible with imperial majesty. So he became contemptible in the eyes of his soldiers. He was hated by the people and despised by the soldiers, so there was soon a conspiracy against him and he was killed.

There remains for us to discuss the character of Maximinus. He was a most warlike individual. The armies had been irritated by the feebleness of Alexander, whom I have already discussed, and so, with him out of the way, they elected Maximinus emperor. But he did not hold on to power for long, for there were two things that made him hateful and contemptible. In the first place, he was of the lowest social status, having once been a shepherd in Thrace (a fact known to everyone, and one that made them all regard him with disdain); in the second, when he was elected emperor he had delayed going to Rome and taking possession of the throne, but had acquired a reputation for terrible cruelty because his representatives, in Rome and throughout the empire, had acted with great ferocity. So everybody was worked up with disdain for his humble origins and agitated with hatred arising from their fear of his ferocity. First Africa rebelled, and then the senate and the whole population of Rome; soon all Italy was conspiring against him. His own army turned against him. They were laying siege to Aquileia, but were finding it hard to take the city, to which was added their distaste for his cruelty. Seeing so many united against him, they lost their fear of him and killed him.

I do not want to discuss Heliogabulus, Macrinus, and Julian, for they were entirely contemptible and fell from power quickly. We can now come to the end of this discussion. I would have you note the rulers of our own day do not face in such an acute form the problem of having to adopt policies that involve breaking the law in order to satisfy their soldiers' appetites; for, although you cannot afford entirely to ignore contemporary soldiers, you can handle them easily. Modern rulers do not face standing armies with long experience of ruling and administering provinces, such as the Roman armies had. But if in those days it was more important to give satisfaction to the soldiers than to the populace, that was because the soldiers were more to be feared than the populace. Now all rulers, with the exception of the sultans of

Turkey and of Egypt, need to be more concerned to satisfy the populace than the soldiers, for the populace are the greater threat. I make an exception of the ruler of Turkey, for at all times he is surrounded by twelve thousand infantry and fifteen thousand cavalry, on whom depends the security and strength of his government. It is essential for him, more than anything else, to retain their loyalty. Similarly, the Sultan of Egypt is entirely at the mercy of his soldiers, so that he, too, must keep their loyalty, no matter what the consequences for the populace may be. And one should note the Sultan of Egypt is in a different position from all other rulers; for he is comparable to the Christian pope, who also cannot be described as either a hereditary or a new ruler. For the sons of the old ruler do not inherit his office and remain in power, but the new ruler is elected by a group who have the authority to appoint him. Since this arrangement has long been in existence, you cannot call the sultan a new ruler, for he faces none of the difficulties faced by those who are new to power. Even though he himself is new to power, the principle of succession is long-established, and ensures his authority is acknowledged as unquestioningly as would be the case if he were an hereditary ruler.

Let us return to our subject. I believe everyone should agree in the light of this discussion that hatred and contempt caused the fall of the emperors we have been considering, and will also understand how it comes about that, with one group of them following one line of policy and the other its opposite, in both groups one ruler was successful and the rest were killed. For it was pointless and dangerous for Pertinax and Alexander, who were new rulers, to try to imitate Marcus, who had inherited power; similarly it was a bad mistake for Caracalla, Commodus, and Maximinus to imitate Severus, for they lacked the strength [*virtù*] that would have been necessary for anyone following in his footsteps. Thus, a new ruler, who has not inherited power, should not follow the example of Marcus, but need not follow that of Severus. He ought to imitate in Severus those features that are essential for him to establish himself securely in power, and in Marcus those features that are effective and win glory for someone who is seeking to preserve a government that has already entrenched itself.

Chapter Twenty: Whether the building of fortresses (and many other things rulers regularly do) is useful or not.

Some rulers, in order to ensure they have a firm grip on power, have disarmed their subjects. Others have divided up the territories over which they rule. Some have positively encouraged opposition to their own authority. Others have set out to win over those who were hostile to them when they first came to power. Some have built fortresses. Others have destroyed them. It is impossible to pass definitive judgment on any of these policies until one considers the particular circumstances that existed in the state where the policy was adopted. Nevertheless, I will talk in general terms in so far as the subject itself permits.

No new ruler, let me point out, has ever disarmed his subjects; on the contrary, when he has found them disarmed, he has always armed them. For, when you arm them, their arms become yours, those who have been hostile to you become loyal, while those who have been loyal remain so, and progress from being your obedient subjects to being your active supporters. Because not every subject can be armed, provided you ensure those who receive arms stand to benefit, you will be more secure in your dealings with the others. When they recognize this diversity of treatment, it will make them all the more obliged to you; while the unarmed will forgive you, for they will recognize it is necessary that those who face more dangers and have more onerous obligations should be better rewarded. But if you take their arms away from those who have been armed, you begin to alienate them. You make it clear you do not trust them, either because you think they are poor soldiers or disloyal. Whichever view they attribute to you, they will begin to hate you. And, since you cannot remain undefended, you will be obliged to rely on mercenary troops, with the consequences we have already discussed. No matter how good they are, they will be unable to defend you against a combination of powerful foreign powers and hostile subjects. So, as I have said, a new ruler who has not inherited power has always formed his own army. There are innumerable examples in history. But when a ruler acquires a new state, which is simply added on to his existing territories, then it is essential to disarm the people, with the sole exception of those who have actively supported you in taking power. And they too, over time, and as opportunity occurs, should be encouraged to become weak and effeminate. You should arrange things so that all the weapons in your new state are in the hands of those of your own troops who were closely associated with you in your old territories.

Our ancestors, particularly those who were thought wise, used to say it was necessary to hold Pistoia by encouraging factional divisions, and Pisa by building fortresses. So, in some of the territory they occupied, they encouraged divisions in order to have better control. This was a sound policy in the days when Italy experienced a balance of power;[86] but I do not think it can be recommended now. For I do not

86. From 1454 to 1494.

believe any good ever comes of internal conflicts. It is certain that when enemy forces approach you run the risk that divided cities will go over to the other side, for the weaker of the two internal factions will attach itself to the invaders, and the stronger will not be able to retain power against enemies within and without the walls.

The Venetians, following, I believe, the same line of thought as our ancestors, encouraged the division of the cities under their control into the two factions of Guelfs and Ghibellines.[87] Although they never allowed the conflicts between them to go so far as bloodshed, they encouraged these tensions so the inhabitants of these cities would be fully occupied with their own internal disagreements and would not unite against their masters. But history shows this policy did not pay off. For, when they were defeated at Vailà,[88] one of the factions quickly plucked up courage and deprived them of all their territories. Such policies, indeed, imply the ruler is weak, for a robust government would never allow such divisions, since you only benefit from them in time of peace, when they enable you to manage your subjects more easily; when war comes, such a policy proves to be misconceived.

There is no doubt rulers become powerful as they overcome the difficulties they face and the opposition they encounter. So fortune, especially when she wants to make a new ruler powerful (for new rulers have more need of acquiring a reputation than ones who have inherited power), makes him start out surrounded by enemies and endangered by threats, so he can overcome these obstacles and can climb higher on a ladder supplied by his enemies. Therefore, many conclude a wise ruler will, when he has the opportunity, secretly foster opposition to his rule, so that, when he has put down his opponents, he will be in a more powerful position.

Rulers, and especially those who are new to power, have sometimes found there is more loyalty and support to be had from those who were initially believed to be opposed to their rule, than from those whom from the start they could count on. Pandolfo Petrucci, ruler of Siena, governed his state by relying more on those who were supposed to be hostile to him than on his supporters.[89] But we cannot discuss this policy in general terms, because its success depends upon circumstances. I will only say those men who have been hostile when a ruler

87. These factions were present in many Italian cities. The Guelfs supported the papacy (and later the French), the Ghibellines the Holy Roman Emperor.
88. In 1509.
89. Petrucci (1450–1512) was effective ruler of Siena from 1487 until his death.

first acquires power, but who belong to those social groups that need to rely on government support in order to maintain their position, can always be won over by the new ruler with the greatest of ease. And they are all the more obliged to serve him faithfully because they know it is essential for them to undo by their actions the negative assessment that was initially made of them. Thus, the ruler can always get more out of them than out of those who, being all too confident of his goodwill, pay little attention to his interests.

And, since it is relevant to our subject, I do not want to fail to point out to rulers who have recently acquired a state through the support of people living within it, that they should give careful consideration to the motives of those who supported them. If they did not give their support out of natural affection for you, but gave it only because they were not happy with their previous government, you will find you can retain their loyalty only with much trouble and effort, for there is no way in which you will be able to keep them happy. If you think about it and consider the record of ancient and modern history, you will realize it will be much easier for you to win the loyalty of those men who were happy with the previous government and were therefore opposed to your seizure of power, than of those who, because they were unhappy with it, became your allies and encouraged you to take power from it.

Rulers have been accustomed, in order to have a more secure grip on their territories, to build fortresses. They are intended to be a bridle and bit for those who plan to rebel against you, and to provide you with a secure refuge in the event of an unexpected attack. I approve of this policy, for it was used by the Romans. Nevertheless, Mr. Niccolò Vitelli, in our own day, had two fortresses in Città di Castello destroyed so he could hold on to that state.[90] Guido Ubaldo, the Duke of Urbino, when he returned to power, having previously been driven into exile by Cesare Borgia, completely destroyed all the fortresses in his territory.[91] He believed that without them it would be harder to deprive him once again of power. The Bentivogli, when they recovered power in Bologna, adopted the same policy.[92]

We must conclude that fortresses are useful or not, depending on circumstances, and that, if they are useful at one time, they may also do you harm at another. We can identify the relevant factors as follows: A ruler who is more afraid of his subjects than of foreign powers should

90. In 1482.
91. In 1503.
92. In 1511.

build fortresses; but a ruler who is more afraid of foreign powers than of his subjects should do without them. The castle of Milan, which was built by Francesco Sforza,[93] has done and will do more damage to the house of Sforza than any other defect in that state. For the best fortress one can have is not being hated by one's subjects; for if you have fortresses, but your subjects hate you, they will not save you, for your subjects, once they have risen in arms, will never be short of foreign allies who will come to their support.

In recent times, there is no evidence that fortresses have been useful to any ruler, except for the Contessa of Forlì, when her husband Count Girolamo died:[94] Because she could take refuge in one she was able to escape the popular uprising, hold out until assistance came from Milan, and retake her state. Circumstances at the time were such that the populace could not get assistance from abroad; but later, even she gained little benefit from her fortresses when Cesare Borgia attacked her, and the populace, still hostile to her, joined forces with the invaders.[95] So, both at first and later, it would have been safer for her not to have been hated by her people than to have fortresses. Consequently, having considered all these factors, I would praise both those who build fortresses and those who do not, but I would criticize anyone who, relying on his fortresses, thought it unimportant that his people hated him.

Chapter Twenty-One: What a ruler should do in order to acquire a reputation.

Nothing does more to give a ruler a reputation than embarking on great undertakings and doing remarkable things. In our own day, there is Ferdinand of Aragon, the present King of Spain. He may be called, more or less, a new ruler, because having started out as a weak ruler he has become the most famous and most glorious of all the kings of Christendom. If you think about his deeds, you will find them all noble, and some of them extraordinary. At the beginning of his reign he attacked Granada, and this undertaking was the basis of his increased power.[96] In the first place, he undertook the reconquest when he had no other problems to face, so he could concentrate upon it. He used

93. In 1450.
94. In 1488.
95. In December 1499.
96. The muslim state of Granada was conquered between 1480 and 1492.

it to channel the ambitions of his Castilian barons, who, because they were thinking of the war, were no threat to him at home. Meanwhile, he acquired influence and authority over them without their even being aware of it. He was able to raise money from the church and from his subjects to build up his armies. Thus, this lengthy war enabled him to build up his military strength, which has paid off since. Next, in order to be able to engage in more ambitious undertakings, still exploiting religion, he practiced a pious cruelty, expropriating and expelling from his kingdom the Marranos:[97] an act without parallel and truly despicable. He used religion once more as an excuse to justify an attack on Africa.[98] He then attacked Italy and has recently[99] invaded France. He is always plotting and carrying out great enterprises, which have always kept his subjects bewildered and astonished, waiting to see what their outcome would be. And his deeds have followed one another so closely that he has never left space between one and the next for people to plot uninterruptedly against him.

It is also of considerable help to a ruler if he does remarkable things when it comes to domestic policy, such as those that are reported of Mr. Bernabò of Milan.[100] It is a good idea to be widely talked about, as he was, because, whenever anyone happened to do anything extraordinary, whether good or bad, in civil life, he found an imaginative way to reward or to punish them. Above all a ruler should make every effort to ensure that whatever he does it gains him a reputation as a great man, a person who excels.

Rulers are also admired when they know how to be true allies and genuine enemies: That is, when, without any reservations, they demonstrate themselves to be loyal supporters or opponents of others. Such a policy is always better than one of neutrality. For if two rulers who are your neighbors are at war with each other, they are either so powerful that, if one of them wins, you will have to fear the victor, or they are not. Either way, it will be better for you to take sides and fight a good fight; for, if they are powerful, and you do not take sides, you will still be preyed on by the victor, much to the pleasure and satisfaction of his defeated opponent. You will have no excuse, no defense, no

---

97. The Marranos were Jews who had been forced to convert to Catholicism. On misinterpretations of this term, see Edward Andrew, "The Foxy Prophet: Machiavelli Versus Machiavelli on Ferdinand the Catholic," *History of Political Thought* 11 (1990), 409–22.

98. In 1509.

99. In 1512.

100. Bernabò Visconti ruled Milan from 1354 to 1385.

refuge. For whoever wins will not want allies who are unreliable and who do not stand by him in adversity; while he who loses will not offer you refuge, since you were not willing, sword in hand, to share his fate.

The Aetolians invited Antiochus to Greece to drive out the Romans.[101] Antiochus sent an ambassador to the Achaeans, who were allies of the Romans, to encourage them to remain neutral; while the Romans urged them to fight on their side. The ruling council of the Achaeans met to decide what to do, and Antiochus's ambassador spoke in favor of neutrality. The Roman ambassador replied: "As for what they say to you, that it would be sensible to keep out of the war, there is nothing further from your true interests. If you are without credit, without dignity, the victor will claim you as his prize."

It will always happen that he who is not your ally will urge neutrality upon you, while he who is your ally will urge you to take sides. Rulers who are unsure what to do, but want to avoid immediate dangers, generally end up staying neutral and usually destroy themselves by doing so. But when a ruler boldly takes sides, if your ally wins, even if he is powerful, and has the ability to overpower you, he is in your debt and fond of you. Nobody is so shameless as to turn on you in so ungrateful a fashion. Moreover, victories are never so overwhelming that the victor can act without any constraint: Above all, victors still need to appear just. But if, on the other hand, your ally is defeated, he will offer you refuge, will help you as long as he is able, and will share your ill-fortune, in the hope of one day sharing good fortune with you. In the second case, when those at war with each other are insufficiently powerful to give you grounds to fear the outcome, there is all the more reason to take sides, for you will be able to destroy one of them with the help of the other, when, if they were wise, they would be helping each other. The one who wins is at your mercy; and victory is certain for him whom you support.

Here it is worth noting a ruler should never take the side of someone who is more powerful than himself against other rulers, unless necessity compels him to, as I have already implied. For if you win, you are your ally's prisoner; and rulers should do everything they can to avoid being at the mercy of others. The Venetians allied with the King of France against the Duke of Milan, when they could have avoided taking sides; they brought about their own destruction.[102] But when you cannot help but take sides (which is the situation the Florentines found themselves

101. 192 B.C. The source is Livy, bk. 35, chs. 48, 49.
102. In 1499.

in when the pope and the King of Spain were advancing with their armies to attack Lombardy)[103] then you should take sides decisively, as I have explained. Do not for a moment think any state can always take safe decisions, but rather think every decision you take involves risks, for it is in the nature of things that you cannot take precautions against one danger without opening yourself to another. Prudence consists in knowing how to assess risks and in accepting the lesser evil as a good.

A ruler should also show himself to be an admirer of skill [*virtù*] and should honor those who are excellent in any type of work. He should encourage his citizens by making it possible for them to pursue their occupations peacefully, whether they are businessmen, farmers, or are engaged in any other activity, making sure they do not hesitate to improve what they own for fear it may be confiscated from them, and they are not discouraged from investing in business for fear of losing their profits in taxes; instead, he should ensure that those who improve and invest are rewarded, as should be anyone whose actions will benefit his city or his government. He should, in addition, at appropriate times of the year, amuse the populace with festivals and public spectacles. Since every city is divided into guilds or neighborhoods, he ought to take account of these collectivities, meeting with them on occasion, showing himself to be generous and understanding in his dealings with them, but at the same time always retaining his authority and dignity, for this he should never let slip in any circumstances.

Chapter Twenty-Two: About those whom rulers employ as advisers.

A ruler's choice as to whom to employ as his advisers is of foremost importance. Rulers get the advisers they deserve, for good rulers choose good ones, bad rulers choose bad. The easiest way of assessing a ruler's ability is to look at those who are members of his inner circle. If they are competent and reliable, then you can be sure he is wise, for he has known both how to recognize their ability and to keep them faithful. But if they are not, you can always make a negative assessment of the ruler; for he has already proved his inadequacy by making a poor choice of adviser.

Nobody who knew Mr. Antonio of Venafro[104] when he was adviser

103. In 1512.
104. Machiavelli did, indeed, know Antonio Giordani of Venafro.

to Pandolfo Petrucci, ruler of Siena, could fail to conclude that Pandolfo was a brilliant man, for how else would he come by such an adviser? For there are three types of brains: One understands matters for itself, one follows the explanations of others, and one neither understands nor follows. The first is best, the second excellent, the third useless. It followed logically that if Pandolfo was not in the first rank, then he was at least in the second. For anyone who can judge the good or evil someone says and does, even if he does not have an original mind, will recognize what his adviser does well and what he does ill, and will encourage the first and correct the second. An adviser cannot hope to deceive such an employer, and will do his best.

But there is one infallible way for a ruler to judge his adviser. When you see your adviser give more thought to his own interests than yours, and recognize everything he does is aimed at his own benefit, then you can be sure such a person will never be a good adviser. You will never be able to trust him, for he who runs a government should never think of his own interests, but always of his ruler's, and should never suggest anything to his ruler that is not in the ruler's interests. On the other hand the ruler, in order to get the best out of his adviser, should consider his adviser's interests, heaping honors on him, enriching him, placing him in his debt, ensuring he receives public recognition, so that he sees that he cannot do better without him, that he has so many honors he desires no more, so much wealth he desires no more, so much status he fears the consequences of political upheaval. When a ruler has good advisers and knows how to treat them, then they can rely on each other; when it is otherwise, either ruler or adviser will suffer.

Chapter Twenty-Three: How sycophants are to be avoided.

I do not want to omit an important subject that concerns a mistake it is difficult for rulers to avoid making, unless they are very wise and good judges of men. My subject is sycophants, who pullulate at court. For men are so easily flattered and are so easily taken in by praise, that it is difficult for them to defend themselves against this plague, and in defending themselves they run the risk of making themselves despicable. For there is no way of protecting oneself against flattery other than by making it clear you do not mind being told the truth; but, when anyone can tell you the truth, then you are not treated with sufficient respect. So a wise ruler ought to find an alternative to flattery and excessive frankness. He ought to choose wise men from among his subjects, and give to them alone freedom to tell him the truth, but only in reply to specific questions he puts to them, not on any subject of their choice. But he ought to ask them about everything, and listen to their replies; then think matters over on his own, in his own way. His response to each of his advisers and their advice should make it apparent that the more freely they talk, the happier he will be. But he should listen to no one who has not been designated as an adviser, he should act resolutely once he has made up his mind, and he should cling stubbornly to his decisions once they have been taken. He who acts otherwise either is rushed into decisions by flatterers or changes his mind often in response to differing advice. Either way, people will form a poor opinion of him.

I want, on this subject, to refer to an example from recent history. The cleric Luca,[105] an adviser to Maximilian, the present emperor, speaking of his sovereign, said that he did not ask for anyone's advice, and that he never did anything the way he wanted to: which was because he did not follow the principles I have just outlined. For the emperor is a secretive man, he keeps things to himself and never asks anyone's advice. But, when his decisions begin to be discovered, which is when they begin to be put into effect, he begins to be criticized by those who are close to him, and, as one might expect, he is persuaded to change his mind. The result is that he undoes each day what he did the day before; that nobody ever knows what he really wants or intends to do; and that one cannot rely upon his decisions.

A ruler, therefore, should always take advice, but only when he wants to, not when others want him to; he should discourage everybody from giving him advice without being asked; but he should be always asking, and, moreover, he should listen patiently to the answers, provided they are truthful. But if he becomes persuaded someone, for whatever reason, is not telling him the truth, he should lose his temper. There are many who think some rulers who have a reputation for being prudent do not really deserve to be thought so, claiming that the rulers themselves are not wise, but that they merely receive good advice. But without doubt they are mistaken. For this is a general rule without exceptions: A ruler who is not himself wise cannot be given good advice. Unless, I should say, he hands over all decisions to one other person and has the good luck to pick someone quite exceptionally prudent. But such an exceptional arrangement will not last long, for the man who takes all the decisions will soon take power. But a ruler who is not wise, if he takes advice from more than one person, will never get the same advice from everyone, nor will he be able to

105. Also known to Machiavelli.

combine the different proposals into a coherent policy unless he has help. His advisers will each think about his own interests, and he will not be able to recognize their bias or correct it. This is how it has to be, for you will find men are always wicked, unless you give them no alternative but to be good. So we may conclude that good advice, no matter who it comes from, really comes from the ruler's own good judgment, and that the ruler's good judgment never comes from good advice.

Chapter Twenty-Four: Why the rulers of Italy have lost their
states.

The policies I have described, if prudently followed, will make a new ruler seem long-established and will rapidly make his power better entrenched than it would be if he had long held office. For the actions of a new ruler are much more closely scrutinized than those of an hereditary ruler; and new rulers, when they are seen to be strong [*virtuose*], attract much more support and make men more indebted to them than do hereditary rulers. For men are much more impressed by what goes on in the present than by what happened in the past; and when they are satisfied with what is happening now, they are delighted and ask for nothing more. So they will spring to a new ruler's defense, provided he plays his part properly. Thus, he will be doubly glorious: He will have begun a new tradition of government, underpinned and ornamented with good laws, good arms, good allies, and good examples; just as he is doubly shamed who, being born a ruler, has lost power through lack of skill in ruling.

And if you consider those Italian rulers who have lost power in recent years, such as the King of Naples, the Duke of Milan, and others, you will find: First, they all had in common an inadequate military preparation, for the reasons I have discussed above at length; second, you will see that some of them either were at odds with their own populace or, if they had the support of the populace, did not know how to protect themselves from the elite; for without these defects they would not have lost states that were strong enough to put an army in the field. Philip of Macedon (not the father of Alexander, but the Philip who was defeated by Titus Quintius)[106] did not have a large state in comparison with the territory controlled by the Romans and the Greeks who attacked him; nevertheless, because he was a military man and a ruler who knew how to treat his populace and how to protect

---

106. Philip V, defeated in 197 B.C.

himself from the elite, he was able to sustain a war against superior forces for several years; and if, at the end, he lost control of several cities, he nevertheless retained his kingdom.

So our own rulers, each of whom had been in power for many years and then lost it, should not blame fortune but their own indolence. For when times were quiet they never once considered the possibility that they might change (it is a common human failing not to plan ahead for stormy weather while the sun shines). When difficult times did come, they thought of flight not of self-defense. They hoped the populace, irritated by the insolence of their conquerors, would recall them to power. This plan is a good one if there is no alternative policy available; but it is stupid to adopt it when there are alternatives. No one would be happy to trip and fall merely because he thought someone would help him back to his feet. Either no one comes to your assistance; or if someone does, you are the weaker for it, for your strategy for self-defense has been ignominious, and your fate has not been in your own hands. No method of defense is good, certain, and lasting that does not depend on your own decisions and your own strength [*virtù*].

Chapter Twenty-Five: How much fortune can achieve in human affairs, and how it is to be resisted.

I am not unaware of the fact that many have held and still hold the view that the affairs of this world are so completely governed by fortune and by God that human prudence is incapable of correcting them, with the consequence that there is no way in which what is wrong can be put right. So one may conclude that there is no point in trying too hard; one should simply let chance have its way. This view has come to be more widely accepted in our own day because of the extraordinary variation in circumstances that has been seen and is still seen every day. Nobody could predict such events. Sometimes, thinking this matter over, I have been inclined to adopt a version of this view myself. Nevertheless, since our free will must not be eliminated, I think it may be true that fortune determines one half of our actions, but that, even so, she leaves us to control the other half, or thereabouts. And I compare her to one of those torrential rivers that, when they get angry, break their banks, knock down trees and buildings, strip the soil from one place and deposit it somewhere else. Everyone flees before them, everyone gives way in face of their onrush, nobody can resist them at any point. But although they are so powerful, this does not mean men, when the waters recede, cannot make repairs and build banks and barriers so that, if the waters rise again, either they will be safely kept within the sluices or at least their onrush will not be so unregulated and destructive. The same thing happens with fortune: She demonstrates her power where precautions have not been taken to resist her [*dove non è ordinata virtù a resisterle*]; she directs her attacks where she knows banks and barriers have not been built to hold her. If you think about Italy, which is the location of all these changes in circumstance, and the origin of the forces making for change, you will realize she is a landscape without banks and without any barriers. If proper precautions had been taken [*s'ella fussi reparata da conveniente virtù*], as they were in Germany, Spain, and France, either the flood would not have had the consequences it had, or the banks would not even have been overwhelmed. And what I have said is enough, I believe, to answer the general question of how far one can resist fortune.

But, turning rather to individuals, note we see rulers who flourish one day and are destroyed the next without our being able to see any respect in which they have changed their nature or their attributes. I think the cause of this is, in the first place, the one we have already discussed at length: A ruler who depends entirely on his good fortune will be destroyed when his luck changes. I also think a ruler will flourish if he adjusts his policies as the character of the times changes; and similarly, a ruler will fail if he follows policies that do not correspond to the needs of the times. For we see men, in those activities that carry them towards the goal they all share, which is the acquisition of glory and riches, proceed differently. One acts with caution, while another is headstrong; one is violent, while another relies on skill; one is patient, while another is the opposite: And any one of them, despite the differences in their methods, may achieve his objective. One also sees that of two cautious men, one will succeed, and the other not; and similarly we see that two men can be equally successful though quite different in their behavior, one of them being cautious and the other headstrong. This happens solely because of the character of the times, which either suits or is at odds with their way of proceeding. This is the cause of what I have described: that two men, behaving differently, achieve the same result, and of two other men, who behave in the same way, one will attain his objective and the other will not. This is also the cause of the fact that the sort of behavior that is successful changes from one time to another. Take someone who acts cautiously and patiently. If the times and circumstances develop in such a way that his behavior is appropriate, he will flourish; but if the times and circumstances change, he will be destroyed for he will continue to behave in the same way. One cannot find a man so prudent he knows how to adapt himself to changing circumstances, for he will either be unable to deviate from that style of behavior to which his character inclines him, or, alternatively, having always been successful by adopting one particular style, he will be unable to persuade himself that it is time to change. And so, the cautious man, when it is time to be headstrong, does not know how to act and is destroyed. But, if one knew how to change one's character as times and circumstances change, one's luck would never change.

Pope Julius II always acted impetuously; the style of action was so appropriate to the times and circumstances in which he found himself that the outcome was always successful. Consider his first attack on Bologna, when Mr. Giovanni Bentivoglio was still alive.[107] The Venetians were not happy about it; nor was the King of Spain; he had discussed such an action with the French, who had reached no decision. Nevertheless, because he was ferocious and impetuous, he placed himself personally at the head of his troops. This gesture made the Spanish and the Venetians hesitate and do nothing: the Venetians out of fear, and the Spanish because they wanted to recover the territories they had lost from the Kingdom of Naples. On the other hand, he dragged the King of France along behind him. For the king saw it was too late to turn back, and he wanted an alliance with him in order to weaken the Venetians, so he concluded he could not deny him the support of French troops without giving him obvious grounds for resentment. So Julius, by acting impetuously, achieved something no other pope, no matter how skillful and prudent, had been able to achieve. For, if he had delayed his departure from Rome until everything had been arranged and the necessary alliances had been cemented, as any other pope would have done, he would never have succeeded. The King of France would have found a thousand excuses, and his other allies would have pointed out a thousand dangers. I want to leave aside his other actions, for they were all similar, and they were all successful. He did not live long enough to experience failure. But, if the times had changed so that it was necessary to proceed with caution, he would have been destroyed. He would never have been able to change the style of behavior to which his character inclined him.

I conclude, then, that since fortune changes, and men stubbornly continue to behave in the same way, men flourish when their behavior suits the times and fail when they are out of step. I do think, however, that it is better to be headstrong than cautious, for fortune is a lady. It is necessary, if you want to master her, to beat and strike her. And

107. In 1506.

one sees she more often submits to those who act boldly than to those who proceed in a calculating fashion. Moreover, since she is a lady, she smiles on the young, for they are less cautious, more ruthless, and overcome her with their boldness.

Chapter Twenty-Six: Exhortation to seize Italy and free her from the barbarians.

Having considered all the matters we have discussed, I ask myself whether, in Italy now, we are living through times suitable for the triumph of a new ruler, and if there is an opportunity for a prudent and bold [*virtuoso*] man to take control of events and win honor for himself while benefiting everyone who lives here. It seems to me so many factors come together at the moment to help out a new ruler that I am not sure if there has ever been a more propitious time for such a man. If, as I said, Moses could demonstrate his greatness [*virtù*] only because the people of Israel were slave in Egypt; if we would never have known what a great man Cyrus was if the Persians had not been oppressed by the Medes; if the remarkable qualities of Theseus became apparent only because the Athenians were scattered abroad: so now, the opportunity is there for some bold Italian to demonstrate his greatness [*virtù*]. For see the conditions to which Italy has been reduced: She is more enslaved than the Jews, more oppressed than the Persians, more defenseless that the Athenians. She has no leader, no organization. She is beaten, robbed, wounded, put to flight: She has experience every sort of injury. Although so far there has been the occasional hint of exceptional qualities in someone, so that one might think he had been ordained by God to redeem Italy, yet later events have shown, as his career progressed, that he was rejected by fortune. So Italy has remained at death's door, waiting for someone who could bind her wounds and put an end to the sack of Lombardy, to the extortion of Tuscany and of the Kingdom of Naples, someone who could heal her sores which long ago became infected. One can see how she prays to God that he will send her someone who will redeem her from this ill treatment and from the insults of the barbarians. One can see every Italian is ready, everyone is eager to rally to the colors, if only someone will raise them high.

At the moment, there is nowhere Italy can turn in her search for someone to redeem her with more chance of success than to your own illustrious family, which is fortunate and resourceful [*virtù*], is favored by God and by the church (indeed the church is now at its command). The undertaking is straightforward, if you keep in mind the lives and the deeds of the leaders I have mentioned. Of course those men were exceptional and marvelous; but, nevertheless, they were only men, and none of them had as good an opportunity as you have at the moment. For their undertakings were not more just than this one, or easier, nor was God more their ally than he is yours. This is truly just: "A war is just if there is no alternative, and the resort to arms is legitimate if they represent your only hope."[108] These circumstances are ideal; and when circumstances are ideal there can be no great difficulty in achieving success, provided your family copies the policies of those I have recommended as your models. Beyond that, we have already seen extraordinary and unparalleled events. God has already shown his hand: The sea has been divided; a cloud has escorted you on your journey; water has flowed out of the rock; manna has fallen from on high. Everything has conspired to make you great. The rest you must do for yourselves. God does not want to have to do the whole thing, for he likes to leave us our free will so we can lay claim to part of the glory by earning it.

There is no need to be surprised that none of the Italian rulers I have discussed has been able to accomplish what I believe your family can achieve, or to be disheartened if during all the wars that have been fought, all the political upheavals that have taken place, it has seemed as if the Italians have completely lost their capacity to fight and win [*la virtù militare*]. This is simply because the traditional way of doing things in Italy is mistaken, and no one has appeared who has known how to bring about change. Nothing does more to establish the reputation of someone who comes new to power than do the new laws and the new institutions he establishes. These, when they are well thought out and noble in spirit, make a ruler revered and admired. In Italy we have the raw materials: You can do anything you wish with them. Here we have people capable of anything [*virtù grande*], all they need are leaders who know what to do. When it comes to fighting one-on-one the Italians prove themselves to be stronger, quicker, cleverer. But when it comes to the clash of armies, the Italians are hopeless. The cause lies in the inadequacy of the leaders. Those who know what to do are not obeyed, and everyone thinks he knows what to do. So far there has been no one who has known how to establish an authority, based on fortune and ability [*virtù*], such that the others will obey him. This is the reason why, through the whole of the last twenty years, during all the wars that have taken place in that time, not a single army consisting solely of Italians has done well. Twenty years ago the Italians were defeated

108. Livy, bk. 9, ch. 1.

at Taro; since then at Alexandria, Capua, Genoa, Vailà, Bologna, Mestre.

So, if your illustrious family wants to follow in the footsteps of those excellent men who liberated the nations to which they belonged, you must, before you do anything else, do the one thing that is the precondition for success in any enterprise: Acquire your own troops. You cannot hope to have more faithful, more reliable, or more skillful soldiers. And if each soldier will be good, the army as a whole will be better still, once they see their ruler place himself at their head and discover he treats them with respect and sympathy. It is necessary, though, to get such an army ready, if we are to be able to defend Italy from the foreigners with Italian strength and skill [*con la virtù italica*].

It is true that the Swiss and Spanish infantries are thought to be intimidating; nevertheless, they both have their defects, so a third force could not only stand up to them, but could be confident of beating them. For the Spanish cannot withstand a cavalry charge; and the Swiss have reason to be afraid of infantry, should they come up against any as determined to win as they are. Thus, we have seen that the Spanish cannot withstand an attack by the French cavalry, and we will see in practice that the Swiss can be destroyed by the Spanish infantry. It is true that we have yet to see the Spanish properly defeat the Swiss, but we have seen an indication of what will happen at the Battle of Ravenna,[109] when the Spanish infantry clashed against the German battalions, for the Germans rely on the same formation as the Swiss. There the Spanish, thanks to their agility and with the help of their bucklers, were able to get underneath the pikes of the Germans and were able to attack them in safety, without the Germans' having any defense. If the cavalry had not driven them off, they would have wiped them out. So, since we know the weakness of each of these infantries, we ought to be able to train a new force that will be able to withstand cavalry and will not be afraid of infantry. To accomplish this we need specially designed weapons and new battle formations. This is the sort of new undertaking that establishes the reputation and importance of a new ruler.

So you should not let this opportunity slip by. Italy, so long enslaved, awaits her redeemer. There are no words to describe with what devotion he would be received in all those regions that have suffered from foreign invasions which have flooded across the land. No words can describe the appetite for revenge, the resolute determination, the spirit of self-sacrifice, the tears of emotion that would greet him. What gates

109. 11 April 1512.

would be closed to him? What community would refuse to obey him?
Who would dare be jealous of his success? What Italian would refuse
to pledge him allegiance? Everyone is sick of being pushed around by
the barbarians. Your family must commit itself to this enterprise. Do
it with the confidence and hope with which people embark on a just
cause so that, marching behind your banner, the whole nation is ennobled. Under your patronage, may we prove Petrarch right:

> Virtue [*virtù*] will take up arms against savagery,
> And the battle will be short.
> For the courage of old is not yet dead
> In Italian hearts.[110]

110. Petrarch, *Italia mia (Ai Signori d'Italia)*, ll. 93–6.

INDEX

Acheans, the, 11
Achilles, 47, 54
Aetolians, the, 10, 11, 69
Agathocles, tyrant of Syracuse (317–289 B.C.), xxi, xxii, xxvi, xxxvi, 28, 30
Agis IV, King of Sparta (244–240 B.C.), xxii
Alba, 19
Albinus, 61
Alexander: Severus, Emperor (222–235), 59, 60, 62–63; VI, Pope (1492–97), xv, 12–14, 22–23, 25–26, 29, 36–37, 54; the Great (356–323 B.C.), 14, 16, 45, 47, 50
Alexandria, 61, 79
Antiochus the Great, war with (192–190), 11, 69
Aquileia, 62
Ardinghelli, papal secretary, 4
Arno, xii, xxxiii
Athens, 17
Austria, xiv

Bacon, Francis, xxxvi, xxxvii
Ballioni: family of, 26
Barbaro, Ermolao, xiv
Baron, Hans, xix, xxiv
Bartolomeo of Bergamo, 41
Bene, Tommaso del, 2
Bentivoglio: Annibale, 57; family of, 57, 66; Giovanni, 12, 57–58, 76
Bertini, Pagolo, 4
Bologna, xii, 23, 37, 57–58, 66, 76, 79
Borgia, Cesare, xv, xvi, xxi, xxii, xxxiii, xxxv, xxxvi, 14, 22, 24–27, 30, 37, 43, 51, 66–67
Braccio, Andrea, 40–41
Brunelleschi, Filippo, xii, xxxiii
Brutus: Lucius Junius, Rome's first consul, xxxv; Marcus Junius, tyrannicide, xi
Buondelmonti, Zanobi, xxiv, xxv
Bussone, Francesco, Count of Carmagnola, 40

Caesar, Julius (d. 44 B.C.), xxii, xxvi, xxx, 47, 50, 61
Camerino, 12

Capua, 17, 79
Caracalla, Antoninus, Emperor (211–217), 59–61, 63
Caravaggio, battle of (1448), 39
Carthage, 17, 28
Casavecchia, Filippo, 1, 3, 4
Castracani, Castruccio, of Lucca (1281–1328), xxvi, xxvii, xxviii
Cataline, xxii
Cesena, 24
Charles VII (1422–61) King of France, 44–45
Charles VIII, King of France (1483–98), xiv, 11, 12, 36, 38, 42
Chiron, 54
Christianity, xi, xii, xxix, xli
Cicero, Marcus Tullius (106–43 B.C.), xxix, xxxiv
Clement VII, Pope, see Medici, Giulio de'
Cleomenes III, King of Sparta (237–221 B.C.), xxii
Colonna, family of, 22–23, 36–37
Columbus, Christopher, xiii
Commodus, Emperor (180–192), 59–61, 63
Conio, Alberigo of, 41
Constantinople, 43
Cyrus, King of the Medes (559–529 B.C.), 18–20, 47, 50, 77

d'Amboise, George, archbishop of Rouen, Cardinal (1498), 14, 27
Dante, xxxiv, 2, 3
Darius I, King of Persia (521–485 B.C.), 21
Darius II, King of Persia (336–330 B.C.), 14
Darius III, King of Persia (336–330 B.C.), 16
David, 44
d'Este, Ercole I, Duke of Ferrara (1471–1505), 7, 12
Diogenes Laertius, xxvii
Dionisotti, Carlo, xvi

Egypt, 19, 62–63, 77
Empire, the Holy Roman, 41

Epaminondas, 39
Euffreducci, Oliverotto, xxi, xxii, 29, 30

Fabius: Maximus Cunctator, 53
Faenza, 12, 22–23
Ferdinand, King of Spain (1474–1516), xv, xviii, xx, 13, 14, 25, 42, 50, 55, 67, 70, 76
Fermo, 29, 30
Ferrara, 36, 42–43: Duke of, *see* d'Este
Florence: constitution of, xiv, xvii, xix, xx, xxiv, xxxii, 33; foreign policy of, xv, xx, 12, 26, 36, 69; military forces of, xiv, xvi, 40, 43; territories of, xii, xiv, 17, 43, 51; *see also* Medici; Savonarola; Soderini
Fogliani, Giovanni, 29, 30
Forlì, 43
Forlì, Countess Caterina Sforza of, xxx, 12, 67
fortune, xxv, xxix, xxx, xxxi, xxxvi, 1, 6, 9, 19, 21–23, 27, 45, 55, 65, 69, 74–78
France: constitution of, xxxi, 15, 16, 58; military forces of, 44–45, 79; territories of, 8; *see also* Louis
Francis: I, King of France (1515–47), xix

Gaeta, 25
Genoa, 12, 79
Germany, 34, 75
Geta, 1
Ghibellines, xxxii, 65
Ginori, Filippo, 2
Giovanna II, Queen of Naples (1414–35), 39
Goliath, 44
Gonzaga, Francesco II, Marquis of Mantua, 12
Goths, the, 45
Gracchi, the brothers, 33
Granada, 67
Greece, xiii, 9–11, 16–17, 21, 33, 43, 69
Guelfs, xxxii, 65
Guicciardini: Antonio, 2; Batista, 2; Francesco, xxxvi

Hamilcar, 28
Hannibal, 52–53
Hawkwood, John, 40
Heliogabulus, Emperor (218–222), 59, 62
Hiero II, King of Syracuse (269–216 B.C.), 20, 44

Imola, 43
Israel, 19, 77

Julian, Emperor (193), 59, 60, 62
Julius II, Pope (1503–13), xv, 7, 26–27, 37, 42–43, 49, 70, 76

Kahn, Victoria, xxii

Leo X, Pope, *see* Medici, Giovanni de'
Livy, xii, xxxiv, xxxvii
Locri, 53
Lombardy, 12–14, 40, 70, 77
Louis: XI, King of France (1461–83), 44; XII, King of France (1498–1515), xv, xviii, 8, 11–14, 23–25, 27, 36–37, 42, 44, 50, 69, 76
Luca [Rainaldi], 72
Lucca, xxvi, xxvii, xxxiii, 12, 26
Lucretius, xii

Macedon, 11
Machiavelli, Giovanni, 2
Macrinus, Emperor (217–218), 59, 62
Mantua, Marquis of, *see* Gonzaga
Marcus Aurelius, Emperor (161–180), 59, 62–63
Marignano, battle of (1515), xix
Marranos, the, 68
Maximilian, Emperor (1493–1519), 72
Maximinus, Emperor (235–238), 59, 60, 62–63
Medes, the, 19, 77
Medici: family of, xi, xv–xviii, xx–xxiii, xxv–xxix, xxxii, 4; Giovanni de' (1475–1521), Pope Leo X (1513–21), xi, xv, xviii, 37; Giuliano de' (1479–1516), xi, xv, xvii–xxi, xxv, xxviii, 3, 4; Giulio de' (1478–1534), Cardinal (1513–1523), Pope Clement VII (1523–1534), xviii, xix, xxv, xxvii; Lorenzo de' (1492–1519), Duke of Urbino (1516–1519), xv, xvii, xix, xxiv, 5
mercenaries, xiv, 38–45, 64
Mestre, 79
Micheletto, xvi
Milan, xiv, xviii, xix, xxvii, 6, 8, 12, 22–23, 36, 39, 41, 46, 67, 68
militia, xvi, 21, 45–46: *see also* Sparta
Modena, xviii
Moses, 18–20, 77

Nabis, tyrant of Sparta (207–192 B.C.), xxi, 33, 56
Najemy, John, xvi
Nantes, 14
Naples, xiv, xv, xviii, xxi, xxiv, 6, 13, 25, 36, 40, 73, 76–77

Niger, 61
Numantia, 17

Oliverotto of Fermo, *see* Euffreducci, Oliverotto
Orco, Remiro d', xxxv, 24
Orsini: family of, 22–24, 26, 30, 36–37, 43–44; Niccolò, 41; Paolo, 24
Ovid, 2

paganism, xxix
Panzano, Frosino da, 2
Parma, xviii
Persians, the, 19, 77
Pertinax, Emperor (192–193), 59, 60, 63
Perugia, 24, 25
Pesaro, 12
Petrarch, 2, 80
Petrucci, Pandolfo, ruler of Siena (1487–1512), 65, 70–71
Philip: II, King of Macedon (360–336 B.C.), xxii, 39, 45; V, King of Macedon (220–159 B.C.), 11, 73
Philopoemen, 47
Piacenza, xviii
Piombino, 12, 25
Pisa, xii, xxxiii, 12, 17, 25–26, 40, 43, 64
Pistoia, 51, 64
Pitigliano, Count of, *see* Orsini, Niccolò
Polybius, xiii
Prato, battle of (1512), xv, 2
Pyrrhus, 16

Quintius: Titus Quintius Flaminius, 73

Ravenna, battle of (1512), xiii, 43, 79
Reggio, xviii
Religion, 28, 36, 68; *see also* Christianity; Paganism; Rome (Church of); Rome (papal state of)
Rimini, 12, 22
Roberto of San Severino, 41
Romagna, xv, 12–14, 23–26, 37, 41, 43, 51
Rome: Church of, 41; papal state of, 12–14, 22, 36–38, 40–41, 63, 68, 77
Romulus, King of Rome (753–715 B.C.), 18–20
Rouen, Cardinal of, *see* d'Amboise
Rucellai: Cosimo, xxiv, xxv; family, xxv, xxvi

Saul, 44
Savonarola, Girolamo (1452–98), xiii, 20
Scali, Giorgio, 33
Scipio Africanus Major, P. Cornelius (234–183 B.C.), 47, 53
Severus, Emperor (193–211), 59–61, 63
Sforza: family of, xxvii, 67; Francesco Maria, Duke of Milan (1450–66), 6, 22, 39–41, 46, 67; Ludovico, Duke of Milan (1494–1500), xiv, 8, 69, 73; Muzio Attendolo (d. 1424), 39
Shakespeare, William, xxxvi
Sicily, 28
Siena, xii, 12, 26, 65, 71
Sinigallia, massacre of, 24, 30
Sixtus IV, Pope (1471–84), 36
Soderini: family of, 4; Piero, Gonfaloniere a Vita (1502–12), xv, xvi, xviii, xxi
Spain: and Naples, 6; military forces of, 79; *see also* Ferdinand
Sparta: empire of, 17, 33; legislators, xxii, 33; militia, 39, 56; *see also* Nabis
Swiss, xiv, xix, 39, 42–44, 79
Syracuse, xxi, 20, 21, 28, 44

Tacitus, Cornelius, xiii
Taro, battle of (1495), 78
Tegrimi, Nicolao, xxvi, xxvii
Thebes, 17, 39
Theseus, founder of Athens, 18–20, 77
Tibullus, 2
Turkey, 9, 15, 16, 43, 62–63
Tuscany, 12, 23, 25, 46, 77

Ubaldo, Guido, Duke of Urbino, 66
Urbino, xix, 23–24, 66

Vailà, battle of (1509), 41, 65, 79
Venafro, Antonio of, 70
Venice: territories of, xiv, 7, 12, 13, 22–23, 36–37, 39, 40, 65, 69, 76
Vettori: Francesco, xi, xiv–xvi, xviii, xix, xxiv, xxv, xli, 1; Paolo, xviii, xix, 1
Vinci, Leonardo da, xxxiii
Virgil, 51
Visconti: Bernabò, ruler of Milan (1354–85), 68; Filippo Maria, Duke of Milan (1412–47), 39
Vitelli: family of, 26, 30, 43–44; Niccolò, 66; Paolo, 29
Vitelli, Vitellozzo, 29, 30

Xenophon, 47